The Poetry of Celia Thaxt

Volume I

Celia Laighton Thaxter was born in Portsmouth, New Hampshire on June 29th, 1835 and spent her childhood years on the Isles of Shoals, initially on White Island, where her father, Thomas Laighton, was a lighthouse keeper, and then the wonderfully named Smuttynose and Appledore Islands.

At sixteen, she married Levi Thaxter, her father's business partner, and moved to the mainland, residing first in Watertown, Massachusetts, at a property his father owned. In 1854, they moved to a house in Newburyport and later, in 1856, acquired their own home near the Charles River at Newtonville.

Celia had two sons, one of whom was Roland, born August 28, 1858, and would become a prominent mycologist who would later teach at Harvard.

Her first published poem was written during this time on the mainland. That poem, "Land-Locked", was first published in the Atlantic Monthly in 1861 and earned her $10. It was to be the beginning of a career that would make her one of America's most popular poets and short story writers.

Her marriage with Levi was not perfect, tensions gradually increased. After 10 years she moved back to the islands and her beloved Appledore Island. The marriage was not over but the separations grew longer as Levi didn't share his wife's love of island life.

Celia became the hostess of her father's hotel, the Appledore House, and many New England literary and artists stayed thee; Ralph Waldo Emerson, Nathaniel Hawthorne, Henry Wadsworth Longfellow, Henry David Thoreau, John Greenleaf Whittier, Sarah Orne Jewett, and the artists William Morris Hunt, Childe Hassam, who painted several pictures of her and watercolorist Ellen Robbins, who painted the flowers in her garden.

Celia was present at the time of the infamous murders on Smuttynose Island, about which she wrote the essay, A Memorable Murder which we have included at the end of this volume of poetry.

William Morris Hunt, a close family friend, trying to recover from a debilitating depression, drowned in late summer 1879, an apparent suicide, three days after finishing his last sketch. Celia bore the horror of discovering the body.

That same year, the Thaxters' bought 186 acres on Seapoint Beach on Cutts Island, Kittery Point, where they built a grand Shingle Style "cottage" called Champernowne Farm. In 1880, they auctioned the Newtonville house, and in 1881, moved to their new home.

In March 1888, her friend and fellow poet Whittier hoped "on that lonesome, windy coast where she can only look upon the desolate, winter-bitten pasture-land and the cold grey sea" she could be comforted by "memories of her Italian travels".

Among Celia's most remembered and best loved poems are "The Burgomaster Gull", "Landlocked", "Milking", "The Great White Owl", "The Kingfisher", and "The Sandpiper".

Celia Thaxter died suddenly on August 25th, 1894 on Appledore Island and is buried not far from her cottage, which later burned down in the 1914 fire that consumed The Appledore House hotel.

Index of Contents

PREFACE

In Volume I of this new edition of the collected writings of Celia Thaxter, great care has been taken to keep to her own arrangement and to the order in which the poems were originally published. In this way they seem to make something like a journal of her daily life and thought, and to mark the constantly increasing power of observation which was so marked a trait in her character. As her eyes grew quicker to see the blooming of flowers and the flight of birds, the turn of the waves as they broke on the rocks of Appledore, so the eyes of her spirit read more and more clearly the inward significance of things, the mysterious sorrows and joys of human life. In the earliest of her poems there is much to be found of that strange insight and anticipation of experience which comes with such gifts of nature and gifts for writing as hers, but as life went on it seemed as if Sorrow were visible to her eyes, a shrouded figure walking in the daylight. Here I and Sorrow sit was often true to the sad vision of her imagination, yet she oftenest came hand in hand with some invisible dancing Joy to a friend's door.

Through the long list of these brief poems (beginning in the earliest book with Land-locked and following through the volumes called Driftweed and The Cruise of the Mystery; all reprinted here with some later verses found together among her papers), one walks side by side in intimate companionship with this sometimes sad-hearted but sincerely glad and happy woman and poet, and knows the springs of her life and the power of her great love and hope. In another volume all her delightful verses and stories for children have been gathered; but one poem, The Sandpiper, seemed to belong to one book as much as to the other, and this has been reprinted in both.

In the volume of her Letters will be found the records of Celia Thaxter's life and so far as it could be told the history of her literary work, while some personal notes by the hand of one of her dearest and oldest friends leave little to be said here. Yet those who have known through her writings alone the islands she loved so much, may care to know how, just before she died, she paid, as if with dim foreboding, a last visit to the old familiar places of the tiny world that was so dear to her. Day after day she called those who were with her to walk or sail; once to spend a long afternoon among the high cliffs of Star Island where we sat in the shade behind the old church, and she spoke of the year that she spent in the Gosport parsonage, and went there with us, to find old memories waiting to surprise her in the worn doorways, and ghosts and fancies of her youth tenanting all the ancient rooms. Once we went to the lighthouse on White Island, where she walked lightly over the rough rocks with wonted feet, and showed us many a trace of her childhood, and sang some quaint old songs, as we sat on the cliff looking seaward, with a touching lovely cadence in her voice, an unforgotten cadence to any one who ever heard her sing. We sat by the Spaniards' graves through a long summer twilight, and she repeated her poem as if its familiar words were new, and we talked of many things as we watched the sea. And on Appledore she showed us all the childish playgrounds dearest to her and to her brothers, — the cupboard in a crevice of rock, the old wells and cellars, the tiny stone-walled enclosures, the worn doorsteps of unremembered houses. We crept under the Sheep rock for shelter out of a sudden gust of rain, we found some of the rarer wild flowers in their secret places. In one of these it thrills me now to remember that she saw a new white flower, strange to her and to the island, which seemed to reach up to her hand. "This never bloomed on Appledore before," she said, and looked at it with grave wonder. "It has not quite bloomed yet," she said, standing before the flower; " I shall come here again; " and then we went our unreturning way up the footpath that led over the ledges, and left the new flower growing in its deep windless hollow on the soft green turf.

It was midsummer, and the bayberry bushes were all a bright and shining green, and we watched a sandpiper, and heard the plaintive cry that begged us not to find and trouble its nest. Under the very rocks and gray ledges, to the far nests of the wild sea birds, her love and knowledge seemed to go. She was made of that very dust, and set about with that sea, islanded indeed in the reserves of her lonely nature with its storms and calmness of high tides, but it seemed as if a little star dust must have been mixed with the ordinary dust of those coasts; there was something bright in her spirit that will forever shine, and light the hearts of those who loved her. It will pass on to a later time in these poems that she wrote of music, of spring and winter, of flowers and birds, and of that northern sea which was her friend and fellow.

S. O. J.

LAND-LOCKED

Black lie the hills; swiftly doth daylight flee;
And, catching gleams of sunset's dying smile,
Through the dusk land for many a changing mile
The river runneth softly to the sea.

O happy river, could I follow thee!
yearning heart, that never can be still!
O wistful eyes, that watch the steadfast hill,
Longing for level line of solemn sea!

Have patience; here are flowers and songs of birds,
Beauty and fragrance, wealth of sound and sight,
All summer's glory thine from morn till night,
And life too full of joy for uttered words.

Neither am I ungrateful; but I dream
Deliciously how twilight falls to-night
Over the glimmering water, how the light
Dies blissfully away, until I seem

OFF SHORE

To feel the wind, sea-scented, on my cheek,
To catch the sound of dusky napping sail
And dip of oars, and voices on the gale
Afar off, calling low, — my name they speak!

Earth! thy summer song of joy may soar
Ringing to heaven in triumph. I but crave
The sad, caressing murmur of the wave
That breaks in tender music on the shore.

OFF SHORE

Rock, little boat, beneath the quiet sky;
Only the stars behold us where we lie, —
Only the stars and yonder brightening moon.

On the wide sea to-night alone are we;
The sweet, bright summer day dies silently,
Its glowing sunset will have faded soon.

Rock softly, little boat, the while I mark
The far off gliding sails, distinct and dark,
Across the west pass steadily and slow.

But on the eastern waters sad, they change
And vanish, dream-like, gray, and cold, and strange,
And no one knoweth whither they may go.

We care not, we, drifting with wind and tide,
While glad waves darken upon either side,
Save where the moon sends silver sparkles down,

And yonder slender stream of changing light,
Now white, now crimson, tremulously bright,
Where dark the lighthouse stands, with fiery crown

Thick falls the dew, soundless on sea and shore:
It shines on little boat and idle oar,
Wherever moonbeams touch with tranquil glow.

The waves are full of whispers wild and sweet;
They call to me, — incessantly they beat
Along the boat from stern to curved prow.

Comes the careering wind, blows back my hair,
All damp with dew, to kiss me unaware,
Murmuring "Thee I love," and passes on.

Sweet sounds on rocky shores the distant rote;
Oh could we float forever, little boat,
Under the blissful sky drifting alone!

EXPECTATION

Throughout the lonely house the whole day long
The wind-harp's fitful music sinks and swells, —
A cry of pain, sometimes, or sad and strong,
Or faint, like broken peals of silver bells.

Across the little garden comes the breeze,
Bows all its cups of flame, and brings to me
Its breath of mignonette and bright sweet-peas,
With drowsy murmurs from the encircling sea.

In at the open door a crimson drift

Of fluttering, fading woodbine leaves is blown,
And through the clambering vine the sunbeams sift,
And trembling shadows on the floor are thrown.

I climb the stair, and from the window lean
Seeking thy sail, love, that still delays;
Longing to catch its glimmer, searching keen
The jealous distance veiled in tender haze.

What care I if the pansies purple be,
Or sweet the wind-harp wails through the slow hours;
Or that the lulling music of the sea
Comes woven with the perfume of the flowers?

Thou comest not! I ponder o'er the leaves,
The crimson drift behind the open door:
Soon shall we listen to a wind that grieves,
Mourning this glad year, dead forevermore.

And, my love, shall we on some sad day
Find joys and hopes low fallen like the leaves,
Blown by life's chilly autumn wind away
In withered heaps God's eye alone perceives?

Come thou, and save me from my dreary thought!
Who dares to question Time, what it may bring?
Yet round us lies the radiant summer, fraught
With beauty: must we dream of suffering?

Yea, even so. Through this enchanted land,
This morning-red of life, we go to meet
The tempest in the desert, hand in hand,
Along God's paths of pain, that seek his feet.

But this one golden moment, — hold it fast!
The light grows long: low in the west the sun,
Clear red and glorious, slowly sinks at last,
And while I muse, the tranquil day is done.

The land breeze freshens in thy gleaming sail!
Across the singing waves the shadows creep:
Under the new moon's thread of silver pale,
With the first star, thou comest o'er the deep.

THE WRECK OF THE POCAHONTAS

I lit the lamps in the lighthouse tower,
For the sun dropped down and the day was dead
They shone like a glorious clustered flower, —
Ten golden and five red.

Looking across, where the line of coast
Stretched darkly, shrinking away from the sea,
The lights sprang out at its edge, — almost
They seemed to answer me!

O warning lights! burn bright and clear,
Hither the storm comes! Leagues away
It moans and thunders low and drear, —
Burn till the break of day!

Good-night! I called to the gulls that sailed
Slow past me through the evening sky;
And my comrades, answering shrilly, hailed
Me back with boding cry.

A mournful breeze began to blow;
Weird music it drew through the iron bars;
The sullen billows boiled below,
And dimly peered the stars;

The sails that flecked the ocean floor
From east to west leaned low and fled;
They knew what came in the distant roar
That filled the air with dread!

Flung by a fitful gust, there beat
Against the window a dash of rain:
Steady as tramp of marching feet
Strode on the hurricane.

It smote the waves for a moment still,
Level and deadly white for fear;
The bare rock shuddered, — an awful thrill
Shook even my tower of cheer.

Like all the demons loosed at last,
Whistling and shrieking, wild and wide,
The mad wind raged, while strong and fast
Boiled in the rising tide.

And soon in ponderous showers, the spray,
Struck from the granite, reared and sprung
And clutched at tower and cottage gray,

Where overwhelmed they clung

Half drowning to the naked rock;
But still burned on the faithful light,
Nor faltered at the tempest's shock,
Through all the fearful night.

Was it in vain? That knew not we.
We seemed, in that confusion vast
Of rushing wind and roaring sea,
One point whereon was cast

The whole Atlantic's weight of brine.
Heaven help the ship should drift our way!
No matter how the light might shine
Far on into the day.

When morning dawned, above the din
Of gale and breaker boomed a gun!
Another! We who sat within
Answered with cries each one.

Into each other's eyes with fear
We looked through helpless tears, as still,
One after one, near and more near,
The signals pealed, until

The thick storm seemed to break apart
To show us, staggering to her grave,
The fated brig. We had no heart
To look, for naught could save.

One glimpse of black hull heaving slow,
Then closed the mists o'er canvas torn
And tangled ropes swept to and fro
From masts that raked forlorn.

Weeks after, yet ringed round with spray
Our island lay, and none might land;
Though blue the waters of the bay
Stretched calm on either hand.

And when at last from the distant shore
A little boat stole out, to reach
Our loneliness, and bring once more
Fresh human thought and speech,

We told our tale, and the boatmen cried:

"'Twas the Pocahontas, — all were lost!
For miles along the coast the tide
Her shattered timbers tossed."

Then I looked the whole horizon round, —
So beautiful the ocean spread
About us, o'er those sailors drowned!
"Father in heaven, " I said, —

A child's grief struggling in my breast, —
"Do purposeless thy children meet
Such bitter death? How was it best
These hearts should cease to beat?

"Oh wherefore? Are we naught to Thee?
Like senseless weeds that rise and fall
Upon thine awful sea, are we
No more then, after all? "

And I shut the beauty from ray sight,
For I thought of the dead that lay below;
From the bright air faded the warmth and light,
There came a chill like snow.

Then I heard the far-off rote resound,
Where the breakers slow and slumberous rolled,
And a subtile sense of Thought profound
Touched me with power untold.

And like a voice eternal spake
That wondrous rhythm, and, "Peace, be still!"
It murmured, "bow thy head and take
Life's rapture and life's ill,

"And wait. At last all shall be clear."
The long, low, mellow music rose
And fell, and soothed my dreaming ear
With infinite repose.

Sighing I climbed the lighthouse stair,
Half forgetting my grief and pain;
And while the day died, sweet and fair,
I lit the lamps again.

A THANKSGIVING

High on the ledge the wind blows the bayberry bright,
Turning the leaves till they shudder and shine in the light;
Yellow St. John's- wort and yarrow are nodding their heads,
Iris and wild-rose are glowing in purples and reds.

Swift flies the schooner careering beyond o'er the blue;
Faint shows the furrow she leaves as she cleaves lightly through;
Gay gleams the fluttering flag at her delicate mast;
Full swell the sails with the wind that is following fast.

Quail and sandpiper and swallow and sparrow are here:
Sweet sound their manifold notes, high and low, far and near;
Chorus of musical waters, the rush of the breeze,
Steady and strong from the south, — what glad voices are these!

O cup of the wild-rose, curved close to hold odorous dew,
What thought do you hide in your heart? I would that I knew!
O beautiful Iris, unfurling your purple and gold,
What victory fling you abroad in the flags you unfold?

Sweet may your thought be, red rose, but still sweeter is mine,
Close in my heart hidden, clear as your dewdrop divine.
Flutter your gonfalons, Iris, the paean I sing
Is for victory better than joy or than beauty can bring.

Into thy calm eyes, Nature, I look and rejoice;
Prayerful, I add my one note to the Infinite voice:
As shining and singing and sparkling glides on the glad day,
And eastward the swift-rolling planet wheels into the gray.

THE MINUTE-GUNS

I stood within the little cove,
Full of the morning's life and hope,
While heavily the eager waves
Charged thundering up the rocky slope.

The splendid breakers! How they rushed,
All emerald green and flashing white,
Tumultuous in the morning sun,
With cheer and sparkle and delight!

And freshly blew the fragrant wind,
The wild sea wind, across their tops,
And caught the spray and flung it far
In sweeping showers of glittering drops.

Within the cove all flashed and foamed
With many a fleeting rainbow hue;
Without, gleamed bright against the sky
A tender wavering line of blue,

Where tossed the distant waves, and far
Shone silver- white a quiet sail;
And overhead the soaring gulls
With graceful pinions stemmed the gale.

And all my pulses thrilled with joy,
Watching the winds 'and waters' strife,
With sudden rapture, — and I cried,
"Oh, sweet is life! Thank God for life!

Sailed any cloud across the sky,
Marring this glory of the sun's?
Over the sea, from distant forts,
There came the boom of minute-guns!

War-tidings! Many a brave soul fled,
And many a heart the message stuns!
I saw no more the joyous waves,
I only heard the minute-guns.

SEAWARD

TO —

How long it seems since that mild April night,
When, leaning from the window, you and I
Heard, clearly ringing from the shadowy bight,
The loon's unearthly cry!

Southwest the wind blew, million little waves
Ran rippling round the point in mellow tune,
But mournful, like the voice of one who raves,
That laughter of the loon!

We called to him, while blindly through the haze
Uprose the meagre moon behind us, slow,
So dim, the fleet of boats we scarce could trace,
Moored lightly just below.

We called, and lo, he answered! Half in fear

We sent the note back. Echoing rock and bay
Made melancholy music far and near,
Sadly it died away.

That schooner, you remember? Flying ghost!
Her canvas catching every wandering beam,
Aerial, noiseless, past the glimmering coast
She glided like a dream.

ROCK WEEDS

Would we were leaning from your window now,
Together calling to the eerie loon,
The fresh wind blowing care from either brow,
This sumptuous night of June!

So many sighs load this sweet inland air,
'T is hard to breathe, nor can we find relief, —
However lightly touched we all must share
This nobleness of grief.

But sighs are spent before they reach your ear;
Vaguely they mingle with the water's rune,
No sadder sound salutes you than the clear,
Wild laughter of the loon.

So bleak these shores, wind-swept and all the year
Washed by the wild Atlantic's restless tide,
You would not dream that flowers the woods hold deal
Amid such desolation dare abide.

Yet when the bitter winter breaks, some day,
With soft winds fluttering her garments' hem,
Up from the sweet South comes the lingering May,
Sets the first wind-flower trembling on its stem;

Scatters her violets with lavish hands,
White, blue, and amber; calls the columbine,
Till like clear flame in lonely nooks, gay bands
Swinging their scarlet bells, obey the sign;

Makes buttercups and dandelions blaze,
And throws in glimmering patches here and there,
The little eyebright's pearls, and gently lays
The impress of her beauty everywhere.

Later, June bids the sweet wild rose to blow;
Wakes from its dream the drowsy pimpernel)
Unfolds the bindweed's ivory buds, that glow
As delicately blushing as a shell.

Then purple Iris smiles, and hour by hour,
The fair procession multiplies; and soon,
In clusters creamy white, the elder-flower
Waves its broad disk against the rising moon.

O'er quiet beaches shelving to the sea
Tall mulleins sway, and thistles; all day long
Flows in the wooing water dreamily,
With subtile music in its slumberous song.

Herb-robert hears, and princess' feather bright,
And goldthread clasps the little skull-cap blue;
And troops of swallows, gathering for their flight,
O'er goldenrod and asters hold review.

The barren island dreams in flowers, while blow
The south winds, drawing haze o'er sea and land;
Yet the great heart of ocean, throbbing slow,
Makes the frail blossoms vibrate where they stand;

And hints of heavier pulses soon to shake
Its mighty breast when summer is no more,
And devastating waves sweep on and break,
And clasp with girdle white the iron shore.

Close folded, safe within the sheltering seed,
Blossom and bell and leafy beauty hide;
Nor icy blast, nor bitter spray they heed,
But patiently their wondrous change abide.

The heart of God through his creation stirs,
We thrill to feel it, trembling as the flowers
That die to live again, — his messengers,
To keep faith firm in these sad souls of ours.

The waves of Time may devastate our lives,
The frosts of age may check our failing breath,
They shall not touch the spirit that survives
Triumphant over doubt and pain and death.

THE SANDPIPER

Across the narrow beach we flit,
One little sandpiper and I,
And fast I gather, bit by bit,
The scattered driftwood bleached and dry.
The wild waves reach their hands for it,
The wild wind raves, the tide runs high,
As up and down the beach we flit, —
One little sandpiper and I.

Above our heads the sullen clouds
Scud black and swift across the sky;
Like silent ghosts in misty shrouds
Stand out the white lighthouses high.
Almost as far as eye can reach
I see the close-reefed vessels fly,
As fast we flit along the beach, —
One little sandpiper and I.

I watch him as he skims along,
Uttering his sweet and mournful cry.
He starts not at my fitful song,
Or flash of fluttering drapery.
He has no thought of any wrong;
He scans me with a fearless eye.
Stanch friends are we, well tried and strong,
The little sandpiper and I.

Comrade, where wilt thou be to-night
When the loosed storm breaks furiously?
My driftwood fire will burn so bright!
To what warm shelter canst thou fly?
I do not fear for thee., though wroth
The tempest rushes through the sky:
For are we not God's children both,
Thou, little sandpiper, and I?

TWILIGHT

September's slender crescent grows again
Distinct in yonder peaceful evening red,
Clearer the stars are sparkling overhead,
And all the sky is pure, without a stain.

Cool blows the evening wind from out the West
And bows the flowers, the last sweet flowers that bloom, —

Pale asters, many a heavy-waving plume
Of goldenrod that bends as if opprest.

The summer's songs are hushed. Up the lone shore
The weary waves wash sadly, and a grief
Sounds in the wind, like farewells fond and brief.
The cricket's chirp but makes the silence more.

Life's autumn comes; the leaves begin to fall;
The moods of spring and summer pass away;
The glory and the rapture, day by day,
Depart, and soon the quiet grave folds all.

O thoughtful sky, how many eyes in vain
Are lifted to your beauty, full of tears!
How many hearts go back through all the years,
Heavy with loss, eager with questioning pain,

To read the dim Hereafter, to obtain
One glimpse beyond the earthly curtain, where
Their dearest dwell, where they may be or e'er
September's slender crescent shines again!

THE SWALLOW

The swallow twitters about the eaves;
Blithely she sings, and sweet and clear;
Around her climb the woodbine leaves
In a golden atmosphere.

The summer wind sways leaf and spray,
That catch and cling to the cool gray wall;
The bright sea stretches miles away,
And the noon sun shines o'er all.

In the chamber's shadow, quietly,
I stand and worship the sky and the leaves,
The golden air and the brilliant sea,
The swallow at the eaves.

Like a living jewel she sits and sings;
Fain would I read her riddle aright,
Fain would I know whence her rapture springs,
So strong in a thing so slight!

The fine, clear fire of joy that steals

Through all my spirit at what I see
In the glimpse my window's space reveals, —
That seems no mystery!

But scarce for her joy can she utter her song;
Yet she knows not the beauty of skies or seas.
Is it bliss of living, so sweet and strong?
Is it love, which is more than these?

O happy creature! what stirs thee so?
A spark of the gladness of God thou art.
Why should we seek to find and to know
The secret of thy heart?

Before the gates of his mystery
Trembling we knock with an eager hand;
Silent behind them waiteth He;
Not yet may we understand.

But thrilling throughout the universe
Throbs the pulse of his mighty will,
Till we gain the knowledge of joy or curse
In the choice of good or ill.

He looks from the eyes of the little child,
And searches souls with their gaze so clear;
To the heart some agony makes wild
He whispers, "I am here."

He smiles in the face of every flower;
In the swallow's twitter of sweet content
He speaks, and we follow through every hour
The way his deep thought went.

Here should be courage and hope and faith;
Naught has escaped the trace of his hand;
And a voice in the heart of his silence saith,
One day we shall understand.

A GRATEFUL HEART

Last night I stole away alone, to find
A mellow crescent setting o'er the sea,
And lingered in its light, while over me
Blew fitfully the grieving autumn wind.

And somewhat sadly to myself I said,
"Summer is gone," and watched how bright and fast
Through the moon's track the little waves sped past, —
"Summer is gone! her golden days are dead."

Eegretfully I thought, "Since I have trod
Earth's ways with willing or reluctant feet,
Never did season bring me days more sweet,
Crowned with rare joys and priceless gifts from God.

"And they are gone: they will return no more."
The slender moon went down, all red and still:
The stars shone clear, the silent dews fell chill;
The waves with ceaseless murmur washed the shore.

A low voice spake: "And wherefore art thou sad?
Here in thy heart all summer folded lies,
And smiles in sunshine though the sweet time dies:
'Tis thine to keep forever fresh and glad! "

Yea, gentle voice, though the fair days depart,
And skies grow cold above the restless sea,
God's gifts are measureless, and there shall be
Eternal summer in the grateful heart.

THE SPANIARDS' GRAVES

AT THE ISLES OP SHOALS

O sailors, did sweet eyes look after you
The day you sailed away from sunny Spain?
Bright eyes that followed fading ship and crew,
Melting in tender rain?

Did no one dream of that drear night to be,
Wild with the wind, fierce with the stinging snow,
When on yon granite point that frets the sea,
The ship met her death-blow?

Fifty long years ago these sailors died:
(None know how many sleep beneath the waves:)
Fourteen gray headstones, rising side by side,
Point out their nameless graves, —

Lonely, unknown, deserted, but for me,
And the wild birds that flit with mournful cry,

And sadder winds, and voices of the sea
That moans perpetually.

Wives, mothers, maidens, wistfully, in vain
Questioned the distance for the yearning sail,
That, leaning landward, should have stretched again
White arms wide on the gale,

To bring back their beloved. Year by year,
Weary they watched, till youth and beauty passed,
And lustrous eyes grew dim and age drew near,
And hope was dead at last.

Still summer broods o'er that delicious land,
Rich, fragrant, warm with skies of golden glow:
Live any yet of that forsaken band
Who loved so long ago?

O Spanish women, over the far seas,
Could I but show you where your dead repose!
Could I send tidings on this northern breeze
That strong and steady blows!

Dear dark-eyed sisters, you remember yet
These you have lost, but you can never know
One stands at their bleak graves whose eyes are wet
With thinking of your woe!

WATCHING

In childhood's season fair,
On many a balmy, moonless summer night,
While wheeled the lighthouse arms of dark and bright
Far through the humid air;

How patient have I been,
Sitting alone, a happy little maid,
Waiting to see, careless and unafraid,
My father's boat come in;

Close to the water's edge
Holding a tiny spark, that he might steer
(So dangerous the landing, far and near)
Safe past the ragged ledge.

I had no fears, — not one;

The wild, wide waste of water leagues around
Washed ceaselessly; there was no human sound,
And I was all alone.

But Nature was so kind!
Like a dear friend I loved the loneliness;
My heart rose glad, as at some sweet caress,
When passed the wandering wind.

Yet it was joy to hear,
From out the darkness, sounds grow clear at last,
Of rattling rowlock, and of creaking mast,
And voices drawing near!

"Is 't thou, dear father? Say!"
What well-known shout resounded in reply,
As loomed the tall sail, smitten suddenly
With the great lighthouse ray!

I will be patient now,
Dear Heavenly Father, waiting here for Thee:
I know the darkness holds Thee. Shall I be
Afraid, when it is Thou?

On thy eternal shore,
In pauses, when life's tide is at its prime,
I hear the everlasting rote of Time
Beating for evermore.

Shall I not then rejoice?
Oh, never lost or sad should child of thine
Sit waiting, fearing lest there come no sign,
No whisper of thy voice!

IN MAY

That was a curlew calling overhead,
That fine, clear whistle shaken from the clouds:
See! hovering o'er the swamp with wings outspread,
He sinks where at its edge in shining crowds
The yellow violets dance as they unfold,
In the blithe spring wind, all their green and gold.

Blithe south- wind, spreading bloom upon the sea,
Drawing about the world this band of haze
So softly delicate, and bringing me

A touch of balm that like a blessing stays;
Though beauty like a dream bathes sea and land,
For the first time Death holds me by the hand.

Yet none the less the swallows weave above
Through the bright air a web of light and song,
And calling clear and sweet from cove to cove,
The sandpiper, the lonely rocks among,
Makes wistful music, and the singing sea
Sends its strong chorus upward solemnly.

Mother Nature, infinitely dear!
Vainly I search the beauty of thy face,
Vainly thy myriad voices charm my ear;
I cannot gather from thee any trace
Of God's intent. Help me to understand
Why, this sweet morn, Death holds me by the hand.

I watch the waves, shoulder to shoulder set,
That strive and vanish and are seen no more.
The earth is sown with graves that we forget,
And races of mankind the wide world o'er
Rise, strive, and vanish, leaving naught behind,
Like changing waves swept by the changing wind.

"Hard-hearted, cold, and blind," she answers me,
"Vexing thy soul with riddles hard to guess!
No waste of any atom canst thou see,
Nor make I any gesture purposeless.
Lift thy dim eyes up to the conscious sky!
God meant that rapture in the curlew's cry.

"He holds his whirling worlds in check; not one
May from its awful orbit swerve aside;
Yet breathes He in this south-wind, bids the sun
Wake the fair flowers He fashioned, far and wide,
And this strong pain thou canst not understand
Is but his grasp on thy reluctant hand."

A SUMMER DAY

At daybreak in the fresh light, joyfully
The fishermen drew in their laden net;
The shore shone rosy purple, and the sea
Was streaked with violet;

And pink with sunrise, many a shadowy sail
Lay southward, lighting up the sleeping bay;
And in the west the white moon, still and pale,
Faded before the day.

Silence was everywhere. The rising tide
Slowly filled every cove and inlet small;
A musical low whisper, multiplied,
You heard, and that was all.

No clouds at dawn, but as the sun climbed higher,
White columns, thunderous, splendid, up the sky
Floated and stood, heaped in his steady fire,
A stately company.

Stealing along the coast from cape to cape
The weird mirage crept tremulously on,
In many a magic change and wondrous shape,
Throbbing beneath the sun.

At noon the wind rose, swept the glassy sea
To sudden ripple, thrust against the clouds
A strenuous shoulder, gathering steadily,
Drove them before in crowds;

Till all the west was dark, and inky black
The level-ruffled water underneath,
And up the wind cloud tossed, — a ghostly rack,
In many a ragged wreath.

Then sudden roared the thunder, a great peal
Magnificent, that broke and rolled away;
And down the wind plunged, like a furious keel,
Cleaving the sea to spray;

And brought the rain sweeping o'er land and sea.
And then was tumult! Lightning sharp and keen,
Thunder, wind, rain, — a mighty jubilee
The heaven and earth between!

Loud the roused ocean sang, a chorus grand;
A solemn music rolled in undertone
Of waves that broke about, on either hand,
The little island lone;

Where, joyful in his tempest as his calm,
Held in the hollow of that hand of his,

I joined with heart and soul in God's great psalm,
Thrilled with a nameless bliss.

Soon lulled the wind, the summer storm soon died;
The shattered clouds went eastward, drifting slow;
From the low sun the rain-fringe swept aside,
Bright in his rosy glow,

And wide a splendor streamed through all the sky;
O'er sea and land one soft, delicious blush,
That touched the gray rocks lightly, tenderly;
A transitory flush.

Warm, odorous gusts blew off the distant land,
With spice of pine-woods, breath of hay new mown,
O'er miles of waves and sea scents cool and bland,
Full in our faces blown.

Slow faded the sweet light, and peacefully
The quiet stars came out, one after one:
The holy twilight fell upon the sea,
The summer day was done.

Such unalloyed delight its hours had given,
Musing, this thought rose in my grateful mind,
That God, who watches all things, up in heaven,
With patient eyes and kind,

Saw and was pleased, perhaps, one child of his
Dared to be happy like the little birds,
Because He gave his children days like this,
Rejoicing beyond words;

Dared, lifting up to Him untroubled eyes
In gratitude that worship is, and prayer,
Sing and be glad with ever new surprise,
He made his world so fair!

REGRET

Softly Death touched her, and she passed away
Out of this glad, bright world she made more fair,
Sweet as the apple-blossoms, when in May
The orchards flush, of summer grown aware.

All that fresh, delicate beauty gone from sight,

That gentle, gracious presence felt no more!
How must the house be emptied of delight,
What shadows on the threshold she passed o'er!

She loved me. Surely I was grateful, yet
I could not give her back all she gave me.
Ever I think of it with vague regret,
Musing upon a summer by the sea:

Remembering troops of merry girls who pressed
About me — clinging arms and tender eyes,
And love, like scent of roses. With the rest
She came, to fill my heart with new surprise.

The day I left them all, and sailed away,
While o'er the calm sea, 'neath the soft gray sky,
They waved farewell, she followed me, to say
Yet once again her wistful, sweet "good-by."

At the boat's bow she drooped; her light-green dress
Swept o'er the skiff in many a graceful fold;
Her glowing face, bright with a mute caress,
Crowned with her lovely hair of shadowy gold:

And tears she dropped into the crystal brine
For me, unworthy — as we slowly swung
Free of the mooring. Her last look was mine,
Seeking me still the motley crowd among.

O tender memory of the dead I hold
So precious through the fret and change of years!
Were I to live till Time itself grew old,
The sad sea would be sadder for those tears.

BEFORE SUNRISE

This grassy gorge, as daylight failed last night,
I traversed toward the west, where, thin and young,
Bent like Diana's bow and silver bright,
Half lost in rosy haze, a crescent hung.

I paused upon the beach's upper edge:
The violet east all shadowy lay behind;
Southward the lighthouse glittered o'er the ledge,
And lightly, softly blew the western wind.

And at my feet, between the turf and stone,
Wild roses, bay berry, purple thistles tall,
And pink herb-robert grew, where shells were strown
And morning-glory vines climbed over all.

I stooped the closely folded buds to note,
That gleamed in the dim light mysteriously,
While, full of whispers of the far- off rote,
Summer's enchanted dusk crept o'er the sea.

And sights and sounds and sea-scents delicate,
So wrought upon my soul with sense of bliss,
Happy I sat as if at heaven's gate,
Asking on earth no greater joy than this.

And now, at dawn, upon the beach again,
Kneeling I wait the coming of the sun,
Watching the looser-folded buds, and fain
To see the marvel of their day begun.

All the world lies so dewy-fresh and still!
Whispers so gently all the water wide,
Hardly it breaks the silence: from the hill
Come clear bird-voices mingling with the tide.

Sunset or dawn: which is the lovelier? Lo!
My darlings, sung to all the balmy night
By summer waves and softest winds that blow,
Begin to feel the thrilling of the light!

Red lips of roses, waiting to be kissed
By early sunshine, soon in smiles will break.
But oh, ye morning-glories, that keep tryst
With the first ray of daybreak, ye awake!

O bells of triumph, ringing noiseless peals
Of unimagined music to the day!
Almost I could believe each blossom feels
The same delight that sweeps my soul away.

O bells of triumph! delicate trumpets, thrown
Heavenward and earthward, turned east, west, no south,
In lavish beauty, who through you has blown
This sweet cheer of the morning with calm mouth?

'T is God who breathes the triumph; He who wrought
The tender curves, and laid the tints divine
Along the lovely lines; the Eternal Thought

That troubles all our lives with wise design.

Yea, out of pain and death his beauty springs,
And out of doubt a deathless confidence:
Though we are shod with leaden cares, our wings
Shall lift us yet out of our deep suspense!

Thou great Creator! Pardon us who reach
For other heaven beyond this world of thine,
This matchless world, where thy least touch doth teach
Thy solemn lessons clearly, line on line.

And help us to be grateful, we who live
Such sordid, fretful lives of discontent,
Nor see the sunshine nor the flower, nor strive
To find the love thy bitter chastening meant.

BY THE ROADSIDE

Dropped the warm rain from the brooding sky
Softly all the summer afternoon;
Up the road I loitered carelessly,
Glad to be alive in blissful June.

Though so gray the sky, and though the mist
Swept the hills and half their beauty hid;
Though the scattering drops the broad leaves kissed,
And no ray betwixt the vapor slid,

Yet the daisies tossed their white and gold
In the quiet fields on either side,
And the green gloom deepened in the old
Walnut-trees that flung their branches wide;

And the placid river wound away
Westward to the hills through meadows fair,
Flower-fringed and starred, while blithe and gay
Called the blackbirds through the balmy air.

Right and left I scanned the landscape round;
Every shape, and scent, and wild bird's call,
Every color, curve, and gentle sound,
Deep into my heart I gathered all.

Up I looked, and down upon the sod
Sprinkled thick with violets blue and bright;

"Surely, 'Through his garden walketh God,'"
Low I whispered, full of my delight.

Like a vision, on the path before,
Came a little rosy, sun-browned maid,
Straying toward me from her cottage door,
Paused, up-looking shyly, half afraid.

Never word she spake, but gazing so,
Slow a smile rose to her clear brown eyes,
Overflowed her face with such a glow
That I thrilled with sudden, sweet surprise.

Here was sunshine 'neath the cloudy skies!
Low I knelt to bring her face to mine;
Sweeter, brighter grew her shining eyes,
Yet she gave me neither word nor sign.

But within her look a blessing beamed;
Meek I grew before it; was it just?
Was I worthy this pure light that streamed?
Such approval, and such love and trust!

Half the flowers I carried in my hands
Lightly in her pretty arms I laid:
Silent, but as one who understands,
Clasped them close the rosy little maid.

Fair behind the honeysuckle spray
Shone her innocent, delightful face!
Then I rose and slowly went my way,
Left her standing, lighting all the place.

While her golden look stole after me,
Lovelier bloomed the violets where I trod;
More divine earth's beauty seemed to be:
"Through his garden visibly walked God."

SORROW

Upon my lips she laid her touch divine,
And merry speech and careless laughter died;
She fixed her melancholy eyes on mine,
And would not be denied.

I saw the west wind loose his cloudlets white

In flocks, careering through the April sky;
I could not sing though joy was at its height,
For she stood silent by.

I watched the lovely evening fade away;
A mist was lightly drawn across the stars;
She broke my quiet dream, I heard her say,
"Behold your prison bars!

"Earth's gladness shall not satisfy your soul,
This beauty of the world in which you live;
The crowning grace that sanctifies the whole,
That, I alone can give."

I heard and shrank away from her afraid;
But still she held me and would still abide;
Youth's bounding pulses slackened and obeyed,
With slowly ebbing tide.

"Look thou beyond the evening star," she said,
"Beyond the changing splendors of the day;
Accept the pain, the weariness, the dread,
Accept and bid me stay! "

I turned and clasped her close with sudden strength,
And slowly, sweetly, I became aware
Within my arms God's angel stood at length,
White-robed and calm and fair.

And now I look beyond the evening star,
Beyond the changing splendors of the day,
Knowing the pain He sends more precious far,
More beautiful, than they.

NOVEMBER

There is no wind at all to-night
To dash the drops against the pane;
No sound abroad, nor any light,
And sadly falls the autumn rain;

There is no color in the world,
No lovely tint on hill or plain;
The summer's golden sails are furled,
And sadly falls the autumn rain.

The earth lies tacitly beneath,
As it were dead to joy or pain:
It does not move, it does not breathe, —
And sadly falls the autumn rain.

And all my heart is patient too,
I wait till it shall wake again;
The songs of spring shall sound anew,
Though sadly falls the autumn rain.

COURAGE

Because I hold it sinful to despond,
And will not let the bitterness of life
Blind me with burning tears, but look beyond
Its tumult and its strife;

Because I lift my head above the mist,
Where the sun shines and the broad breezes blow,
By every ray and every raindrop kissed
That God's love doth bestow;

Think you I find no bitterness at all?
No burden to be borne, like Christian's pack?
Think you there are no ready tears to fall
Because I keep them back?

Why should I hug life's ills with cold reserve,
To curse myself and all who love me? Nay!
A thousand times more good than I deserve
God gives me every day.

And in each one of these rebellious tears,
Kept bravely back, He makes a rainbow shine;
Grateful I take his slightest gift, no fears
Nor any doubts are mine.

Dark skies must clear, and when the clouds are past,
One golden day redeems a weary year;
Patient I listen, sure that sweet at last
Will sound his voice of cheer.

Then vex me not with chiding. Let me be.
I must be glad and grateful to the end.
I grudge you not your cold and darkness, — me
The powers of light befriend.

REMEMBERANCE

Fragrant and soft the summer wind doth blow.
Weary I lie, with heavy, half-shut eyes,
And watch, while wistful thoughts within me rise,
The curtain idly swaying to and fro.

There comes a sound of household toil from far,
A woven murmur: voices shrill and sweet,
Clapping of doors, and restless moving feet,
And tokens faint of fret, and noise, and jar.

Without, the broad earth shimmers in the glare,
Through the clear noon high rides the blazing sun,
The birds are hushed; the cricket's chirp alone
With tremulous music cleaves the drowsy air.

I think, — "Past the gray rocks the wavelets run;
The gold-brown seaweed drapes the ragged ledge;
And brooding, silent, at the water's edge
The white gull sitteth, shining in the sun."

SONG

We sail toward evening's lonely star
That trembles in the tender blue;
One single cloud, a dusky bar,
Burnt with dull carmine through and through,
Slow smouldering in the summer sky,
Lies low along the fading west.
How sweet to watch its splendors die,
Wave-cradled thus and wind-caressed!

The soft breeze freshens, leaps the spray
To kiss our cheeks, with sudden cheer;
Upon the dark edge of the bay
Lighthouses kindle, far and near,
And through the warm deeps of the sky
Steal faint star- clusters, while we rest
In deep refreshment, thou and I,
Wave-cradled thus and wind-caressed.

How like a dream are earth and heaven,

Star- beam and darkness, sky and sea;
Thy face, pale in the shadowy even,
Thy quiet eyes that gaze on me!
Oh, realize the moment's charm,
Thou dearest! we are at life's best,
Folded in God's encircling arm,
Wave-cradled thus and wind-caressed.

A TRYST

From out the desolation of the North
An iceberg took its way,
From its detaining comrades breaking forth,
And traveling night and day.

At whose command? Who bade it sail the deep
With that resistless force?
Who made the dread appointment it must keep?
Who traced its awful course?

To the warm airs that stir in the sweet South,
A good ship spread her sails;
Stately she passed beyond the harbor's mouth,
Chased by the favoring gales;

And on her ample decks a happy crowd
Bade the fair land good-by;
Clear shone the day, with not a single cloud
In all the peaceful sky.

Brave men, sweet women, little children bright,
For all these she made room,
And with her freight of beauty and delight
She went to meet her doom.

Storms buffeted the iceberg, spray was swept
Across its loftiest height;
Guided alike by storm and calm, it kept
Its fatal path aright.

Then warmer waves gnawed at its crumbling base,
As if in piteous plea;
The ardent sun sent slow tears down its face,
Soft flowing to the sea.

Dawn kissed it with her tender rose tints, Eve

Bathed it in violet,
The wistful color o'er it seemed to grieve
With a divine regret.

Whether Day clad its clefts in rainbows dim
And shadowy as a dream,
Or Night through lonely spaces saw it swim
White in the moonlight's gleam,

Ever Death rode upon its solemn heights,
Ever his watch he kept;
Cold at its heart through changing days and nights
Its changeless purpose slept.

And where afar a smiling coast it passed,
Straightway the air grew chill;
Dwellers thereon perceived a bitter blast,
A vague report of ill.

Like some imperial creature, moving slow,
Meanwhile, with matchless grace,
The stately ship, unconscious of her foe,
Drew near the trysting place.

For still the prosperous breezes followed her,
And half the voyage was o'er;
In many a breast glad thoughts began to stir
Of lands that lay before.

And human hearts with longing love were dumb,
That soon should cease to beat,
Thrilled with the hope of meetings soon to come,
And lost in memories sweet.

Was not the weltering waste of water wide
Enough for both to sail?
What drew the two together o'er the tide,
Fair ship and iceberg pale?

There came a night with neither moon nor star,
Clouds draped the sky in black;
With fluttering canvas reefed at every spar,
And weird fire in her track,

The ship swept on; a wild wind gathering fast
Drove her at utmost speed.
Bravely she bent before the fitful blast
That shook her like a reed.

O helmsman, turn thy wheel! Will no surmise
Cleave through the midnight drear?
No warning of the horrible surprise
Reach thine unconscious ear?

She rushed upon her ruin. Not a flash
Broke up the waiting dark;
Dully through wind and sea one awful crash
Sounded, with none to mark.

Scarcely her crew had time to clutch despair,
So swift the work was done:
Ere their pale lips could frame a speechless prayer,
They perished, every one!

IMPRISONED

Lightly she lifts the large, pure, luminous shell,
Poises it in her strong and shapely hand.
"Listen," she says, "it has a tale to tell,
Spoken in language you may understand."

Smiling, she holds it at my dreaming ear:
The old, delicious murmur of the sea
Steals like enchantment through me, and I hear
Voices like echoes of eternity.

She stirs it softly. Lo, another speech!
In one of its dim chambers, shut from sight,
Is sealed the water that has kissed the beach
Where the far Indian Ocean leaps in light.

Those laughing ripples, hidden evermore
In utter darkness, plaintively repeat
Their lapsing on the glowing tropic shore,
In melancholy whispers low and sweet.

O prisoned wave that may not see the sun!
voice that never may be comforted!
You cannot break the web that Fate has spun;
Out of your world are light and gladness fled.

The red dawn nevermore shall tremble far
Across the leagues of radiant brine to you;
You shall not sing to greet the evening star,

Nor dance exulting under heaven's clear blue.

Inexorably woven is the weft
That shrouds from you all joy but memory;
Only this tender, low lament is left
Of all the sumptuous splendor of the sea.

PRESAGE

If, some day, I should seek those eyes
So gentle now, — and find the strange,
Pale shadow of a coming change,
To chill me with a sad surprise;

Shouldst thou recall what thou hast given,
And turn me slowly cold and dumb,
And thou thyself again become
Remote as any star in heaven;

Would the sky ever seem again
Perfectly clear? Would the serene,
Sweet face of nature steal between
This grief and me, to dull its pain?

Oh not for many a weary day
Would sorrow soften to regret,
And many a sun would rise and set
Ere I, with cheerful heart, could say:

"All undeserved it came. To-day,
God takes it back again, because
Too beautiful a thing it was
For such as I to keep for aye."

And ever, through the coming years,
My star, remote in happy skies,
Would seem more heavenly fair through eyes
Yet tremulous with unfallen tears.

MIDSUMMER MIDNIGHT

The wide, still, moonlit water miles away
Stretches in lonely splendor. Whispers creep
About us from the midnight wind, and play

Among the flowers that breathe so sweet in sleep;
A soft touch sways the milk-white, stately phlox,
And on its slender stem the poppy rocks.

Fair faces turn to watch the dusky sea,
And clear eyes brood upon the path of light
The white moon makes, the while deliciously,
Like some vague, tender memory of delight,
Or like some half remembered, dear regret,
Rises the odor of the mignonette.

Midsummer glories, moonlight, flowers asleep,
And delicate perfume, mystic winds that blow
Soft-breathing, full of balm, and the great deep
In leagues of shadow swaying to and fro;
And loving human thought to mark it all,
And human hearts that to each other call;

Needs the enchantment of the summer night
Another touch to make it perfect? Hark!
What sudden shaft of sound, like piercing light,
Strikes on the ear athwart the moonlit dark?
Like some keen shock of joy is heard within
The wondrous music of the violin.

It is as if dumb Nature found a voice,
And spoke with power, though in an unknown tongue.
What kinship has the music with the noise
Of waves, or winds, or with the flowers, slow-swung
Like censers to and fro upon the air,
Or with the shadow, or the moonlight fair?

And yet it seems some subtile link exists,
We know not how. And over every phase
Of thought and feeling wandering as it lists,.
Playing upon us as the west- wind plays
Over the wind-harp, the subduing strain
Sweeps with resistless power of joy and pain.

Slow ebbs the golden tide, and all is still.
Ask the magician at whose touch awoke
That mighty, penetrating, prisoned will,
The matchless voice that so divinely spoke,
Kindling to fresher life the listening soul,
What daring thought such fire from heaven stole?

He cannot tell us how the charm was wrought,
Though in his hand he holds the potent key,

Nor read the spell that to the sweet night brought
This crown of rapture and of mystery,
And lifted every heart, and drew away
All trace of worldliness that marred the day.

But every head is bowed. We watch the sea
With other eyes, as if some hint of bliss
Spoke to us, through the yearning melody,
Of glad new worlds, of brighter lives than this;
While still the milk-white, stately phlox waves slow.
And drowsily the poppy rocks below.

APRIL DAYS

Oh the sweet, sweet lapsing of the tide,
Through the still hours of the golden afternoon!
In the warm, red sunshine, far and wide,
Falling soft as in the crowning days of June!

Calls the gray sandpiper from the quiet shore,
Weave the swallows light and music through the air,
Chants the sparrow all his pleasure o'er and o'er,
Sings and smiles the Spring, and sparkles everywhere.

Well I know that death and pain to all are near,
That, save sorrow, naught is certain this world gives;
Yet my heart stirs with the budding of the year,
And rejoices still with everything that lives.

Fold me then, O south-wind! God is good.
Gladly, gratefully I take thy sweet caress.
Call, sandpiper, from thy solitude,
Every sight and sound has power to bless.

Oh the sweet, sweet lapsing of the tide,
Through the still hours of the golden afternoon!
Nor death, nor pain, nor sorrow shall abide,
For God blesses all his children, late or soon.

HEARTBREAK HILL

In Ipswich town, not far from the sea,
Rises a hill which the people call
Heartbreak Hill, and its history

Is an old, old legend, known to all.

The self-same dreary, worn-out tale
Told by all peoples in every clime,
Still to be told till the ages fail,
And there comes a pause in the march of Time.

It was a sailor who won the heart
Of an Indian maiden, lithe and young;
And she saw him over the sea depart,
While sweet in her ear his promise rung;

For he cried, as he kissed her wet eyes dry,
"I 'll come back, sweetheart; keep your faith!"
She said, "I will watch while the moons go by:"
Her love was stronger than life or death.

So this poor dusk Ariadne kept
Her watch from the hilltop rugged and steep;
Slowly the empty moments crept
While she studied the changing face of the deep,

Fastening her eyes upon every speck
That crossed the ocean within her ken;
Might not her lover be walking the deck,
Surely and swiftly returning again?

The Isles of Shoals loomed, lonely and dim,
In the northeast distance far and gray,
And on the horizon's uttermost rim
The low rock heap of Boon Island lay.

And north and south and west and east
Stretched sea and land in the blinding light,
Till evening fell, and her vigil ceased,
And many a hearth- glow lit the night,

To mock those set and glittering eyes
Fast growing wild as her hope went out.
Hateful seemed earth, and the hollow skies,
Like her own heart, empty of aught but doubt.

Oh, but the weary, merciless days,
With the sun above, with the sea afar, —
No change in her fixed and wistful gaze
From the morning-red to the evening star!

Oh, the winds that blew, and the birds that sang,

The calms that smiled, and the storms that rolled,
The bells from the town beneath, that rang
Through the summer's heat and the winter's cold!

The flash of the plunging surges white,
The soaring gull's wild, boding cry, —
She was weary of all; there was no delight
In heaven or earth, and she longed to die.

What was it to her though the Dawn should paint
With delicate beauty skies and seas?
But the sweet, sad sunset splendors faint
Made her soul sick with memories:

Drowning in sorrowful purple a sail
In the distant east, where shadows grew,
Till the twilight shrouded it, cold and pale,
And the tide of her anguish rose anew.

Like a slender statue carved of stone
She sat, with hardly motion or breath.
She wept no tears and she made no moan,
But her love was stronger than life or death.

He never came back! Yet faithful still,
She watched from the hilltop her life away.
And the townsfolk christened it Heartbreak Hill,
And it bears the name to this very day.

THE SONG-SPAKKOW

In this sweet, tranquil afternoon of spring,
While the low sun declines in the clear west,
I sit and hear the blithe song-sparrow sing
His strain of rapture not to be suppressed;
Pondering life's problem strange, while death draws near,
I listen to his dauntless song of cheer.

His shadow flits across the quiet stone:
Like that brief transit is my space of days;
For, like a flower's faint perfume, youth is flown
Already, and there rests on all life's ways
A dimness; closer my beloved I clasp,
For all dear things seem slipping from my grasp.

Death touches all; the light of loving eyes   .

Goes out in darkness, comfort is withdrawn;
Lonely, and lonelier still the pathway lies,
Going toward the fading sunset from the dawn:
Yet hark! while those fine notes the silence break,
As if all trouble were some grave mistake!

Thou little bird, how canst thou thus rejoice,
As if the world had known nor sin nor curse?
God never meant to mock us with that voice!
That is the key-note of the universe,
That song of perfect trust, of perfect cheer,
Courageous, constant, free of doubt or fear.

My little helper, ah, my comrade sweet,
My old companion in that far-off time
When on life's threshold childhood's winged feet
Danced in the sunrise! Joy was at its prime
When all my heart responded to thy song,
Unconscious of earth's discords harsh and strong.

Now, grown aweary, sad with change and loss,
With the enigma of myself dismayed;
Poor, save in deep desire to bear the cross
God's hand on his defenseless creatures laid,
With patience, — here I sit this eve of spring,
And listen with bowed head, while thou dost sing.

And slowly all my soul with comfort fills,
And the old hope revives and courage grows;
Up the deserted shore a fresh tide thrills,
And like a dream the dark mood melts and goes,
And with thy joy again will I rejoice:
God never meant to mock us with that voice!

IN KITTERY CHURCHYARD

"Mary, wife of Charles Chauncy, died April 23, 1758, in the 24th year of her age."

Crushing the scarlet strawberries in the grass,
I kneel to read the slanting stone. Alas!
How sharp a sorrow speaks! A hundred years
And more have vanished, with their smiles and tears,
Since here was laid, upon an April day,
Sweet Mary Chauncy in the grave away, —
A hundred years since here her lover stood
Beside her grave in such despairing mood,

And yet from out the vanished past I hear
His cry of anguish sounding deep and clear
And all my heart with pity melts, as though
To-day's bright sun were looking on his woe.
"Of such a wife, righteous Heaven! bereft,
What joy for me, what joy on earth is left?
Still from my inmost soul the groans arise,
Still flow the sorrows ceaseless from mine eyes."

Alas, poor tortured soul! I look away
From the dark stone, — how brilliant shines the day!
A low wall, over which the roses shed
Their perfumed petals, shuts the quiet dead
Apart a little, and the tiny square
Stands in the broad and laughing field so fair,
And gay green vines climb o'er the rough stone wall,
And all about the wild birds flit and call,
And but a stone's throw southward, the blue sea
Rolls sparkling in and sings incessantly.
Lovely as any dream the peaceful place,
And scarcely changed since on her gentle face
For the last time on that sad April day
He gazed, and felt, for him, all beauty lay
Buried with her forever. Dull to him
Looked the bright world through eyes with tears so dim!

"I soon shall follow the same dreary way
That leads and opens to the coasts of day."
His only hope! But when slow time had dealt
Firmly with him and kindly, and he felt
The storm and stress of strong and piercing pain
Yielding at last, and he grew calm again,
Doubtless he found another mate before
He followed Mary to the happy shore!
But none the less his grief appeals to me
Who sit and listen to the singing sea
This matchless summer day, beside the stone
He made to echo with his bitter moan,
And in my eyes I feel the foolish tears
For buried sorrow, dead a hundred years!

AT THE BREAKERS' EDGE

Through the wide sky thy north wind's thunder roars
Resistless, till no cloud is left to flee,
And down the clear, cold heaven unhindered pours

Thine awful moonlight on the winter sea.

The vast, black, raging spaces, torn and wild,
With an insensate fury answer back
To the gale's challenge; hurrying breakers, piled
Each over each, roll through the glittering track.

I shudder in the terror of thy cold,
As buffeted by the fierce blast I stand,
Watching that shining path of bronzed gold,
With solemn, shadowy rocks on either hand;

While at their feet, ghastly and white as death,
The cruel, foaming billows plunge and rave,
O Father! where art Thou? My feeble breath
Cries to Thee through the storm of wind and wave.

The cry of all thy children since the first
That walked thy planets' myriad paths among;
The cry of all mankind whom doubt has cursed,
In every clime, in every age and tongue.

Thou art the cold, the swift fire that consumes;
Thy vast, unerring forces never fail;
And Thou art in the frailest flower that blooms,
As in the breath of this tremendous gale.

Yet, though thy laws are clear as light, and prove
Thee changeless, ever human weakness craves
Some deeper knowledge for our human love
That looks with sad eyes o'er its wastes of graves,

And hungers for the dear hands softly drawn,
One after one, from out our longing grasp.
Dost Thou reach out for them? In the sweet dawn
Of some new world thrill they within thy clasp?

Ah! what am I, thine atom, standing here
In presence of thy pitiless elements,
Daring to question thy great silence drear,
No voice may break to lighten our suspense!

Thou only, infinite Patience, that endures
Forever! Blind and dumb I cling to Thee.
Slow glides the bitter night, and silent pours
Thine awful moonlight on the winter sea.

"FOR THOUGHTS"

A pansy on his breast she laid,
Splendid, and dark with Tyrian dyes;
"Take it, 'tis like your tender eyes,
Deep as the midnight heaven," she said.

The rich rose mantling in her cheek,
Before him like the dawn she stood,
Pausing upon Life's height, subdued,
Yet triumphing, both proud and meek.

And white as winter stars, intense
With steadfast fire, his brilliant face
Bent toward her with an eager grace,
Pale with a rapture half suspense.

"You give me then a thought, Sweet!"
He cried, and kissed the purple flower,
And bowed by Love's resistless power,
Trembling he sank before her feet.

She crowned his beautiful bowed head
With one caress of her white hand;
"Rise up, my flower of all the land,
For all my thoughts are yours," she said.

WHEREFORE

Black sea, black sky! A ponderous steamship driving
Between them, laboring westward on her way,
And in her path a trap of Death's contriving
Waiting remorseless for its easy prey.

Hundreds of souls within her frame lie dreaming,
Hoping and fearing, longing for the light:
With human life and thought and feeling teeming,
She struggles onward through the starless night.

Upon her furnace fires fresh fuel flinging,
The swarthy firemen grumble at the dust
Mixed with the coal — when suddenly upspringing,
Swift through the smoke-stack like a signal thrust,

Flares a red flame, a dread illumination!
A cry, — a tumult! Slowly to her helm
The vessel yields, 'mid shouts of acclamation,
And joy and terror all her crew o'erwhelm;

For looming from the blackness drear before them
Discovered is the iceberg — hardly seen,
Its ghastly precipices hanging o'er them,
Its reddened peaks, with dreadful chasms between,

Ere darkness swallows it again! and veering
Ont of its track the brave ship onward steers,
Just grazing ruin. Trembling still, and fearing,
Her grateful people melt in prayers and tears.

Is it a mockery, their profound thanksgiving?
Another ship goes shuddering to her doom
Unwarned, that very night, with hopes as living
With freight as precious, lost amid the gloom,

With not a ray to show the apparition
Waiting to slay her, none to cry " Beware!"
Rushing straight onward headlong to perdition,
And for her crew no time vouchsafed for prayer.

Could they have stormed Heaven's gate with anguished praying,
It would not have availed a feather's weight
Against their doom. Yet were they disobeying
No law of God, to beckon such a fate.

And do not tell me the Almighty Master
Would work a miracle to save the one,
And yield the other up to dire disaster,
By merely human justice thus outdone!

Vainly we weep and wrestle with our sorrow —
We cannot see his roads, they lie so broad:
But his eternal day knows no to-morrow,
And life and death are all the same with God.

GUENDOLEN

She is so fair, I thought, so dear and fair!
Maidenly beautiful from head to feet,
With pensive profile delicate and sweet,
And Titian's color in her sunny hair.

So fair, I thought, rejoicing even to note
The little flexible, transparent wrist,
The purple of the gold-clasped amethyst
That glittered at her white and slender throat;

The tiny ear, curled like a rosy shell;
The gentle splendor of the wide brown eyes,
Deep, lustrous, tender, clear as morning skies;
The full, sad lips, — the voice that like a bell

Rang thrilling with a music sweet and wild,
High, airy- pure as fluting of the fays,
Or bird-notes in the early summer days,
And joyous as the laughter of a child.

Dearest, has Heaven aught to give thee more?
I thought, the while I watched her changing face,
Heard her fine tones, and marked her gestures' grace, —
Yea, one more gift is left, all gifts hefore.

We go our separate ways on earth, and pain,
God's shaping chisel, waits us as the rest,
With nobler charm thy beauty to invest,
And make thee lovelier ere we meet again.

THE WATCH OF BOON ISLAND

They crossed the lonely and lamenting sea;
Its moaning seemed but singing. "Wilt thou dare,"
He asked her, " brave the loneliness with me? "
"What loneliness," she said, "if thou art there?"

Afar and cold on the horizon's rim
Loomed the tall lighthouse, like a ghostly sign;
They sighed not as the shore behind grew dim,
A rose of joy they bore across the brine.

They gained the barren rock, and made their home
Among the wild waves and the sea-birds wild;
The wintry winds blew fierce across the foam,
But in each other's eyes they looked and smiled.

Aloft the lighthouse sent its warnings wide,
Fed by their faithful hands, and ships in sight
With joy beheld it, and on land men cried,

"Look, clear and steady burns Boon Island light!"

And, while they trimmed the lamp with busy hands,
"Shine far and through the dark, sweet light!" they cried;
"Bring safely back the sailors from all lands
To waiting love, — wife, mother, sister, bride! "

No tempest shook their calm, though many a storm
Tore the vexed ocean into furious spray;
No chill could find them in their Eden warm,
And gently Time lapsed onward day by day.

Said I no chill could find them! There is one
Whose awful footfalls everywhere are known,
With echoing sobs, who chills the summer sun,
And turns the happy heart of youth to stone;

Inexorable Death, a silent guest
At every hearth, before whose footsteps flee
All joys, who rules the earth, and, without rest,
Roams the vast shuddering spaces of the sea.

Death found them; turned his face and passed her by,
But laid a finger on her lover's lips,
And there was silence. Then the storm ran high,
And tossed and troubled sore the distant ships.

Nay, who shall speak the terrors of the night,
The speechless sorrow, the supreme despair?
Still like a ghost she trimmed the waning light,
Dragging her slow weight up the winding stair.

With more than oil the saving lamp she fed,
While lashed to madness the wild sea she hear do
She kept her awful vigil with the dead,
And God's sweet pity still she ministered.

O sailors, hailing loud the cheerful beam,
Piercing so far the tumult of the dark,
A radiant star of hope, you could not dream
What misery there sat cherishing that spark!

Three times the night, too terrible to bear,
Descended, shrouded in the storm. At last
The sun rose clear and still on her despair,
And all her striving to the winds she cast,

And bowed her head and let the light die out,

For the wide sea lay calm as her dead love.
When evening fell, from the far land, in doubt,
Vainly to find that faithful star men strove.

Sailors and landsmen look, and women's eyes,
For pity ready, search in vain the night,
And wondering neighbor unto neighbor cries,
"Now what, think you, can ail Boon Island light?"

Out from the coast toward her high tower they sailed;
They found her watching, silent, by her dead,
A shadowy woman, who nor wept, nor wailed,
But answered what they spake, till all was said.

They bore the dead and living both away.
With anguish time seemed powerless to destroy
She turned, and backward gazed across the bay, —
Lost in the sad sea lay her rose of joy.

BEETHOVEN

I

O sovereign Master! stern and splendid power,
That calmly dost both Time and Death defy;
Lofty and lone as mountain peaks that tower,
Leading our thoughts up to the eternal sky:
Keeper of some divine, mysterious key,
Raising us far above all human care,
Unlocking awful gates of harmony
To let heaven's light in on the world's despair;
Smiter of solemn chords that still command
Echoes in souls that suffer and aspire,
In the great moment while we hold thy hand,
Baptized with pain and rapture, tears and fire,
God lifts our saddened foreheads from the dust,
The everlasting God, in whom we trust!

II

O stateliest! who shall speak thy praise, who find
A fitting word to utter before thee?
Thou lonely splendor, thou consummate mind,
Who marshalest thy hosts in majesty;
Thy shadowy armies of resistless thought,
Thy subtile forces drawn from Nature's heart,
Thy solemn breathing, mighty music, wrought

Of life and death — a miracle thou art!
The restless tides of human life that swing
In stormy currents, thou dost touch and sway;
Deep tones within us answer, shuddering,
At thy resounding voice — we cast away
All our unworthiness, made strong by thee,
Thou great uplifter of humanity!

III
And was it thus the master looked, think you?
Is this the painter's fancy? Who can tell!
These strong and noble outlines should be true:
On the broad brow such majesty should dwell.
Yea, and these deep, indomitable eyes
Are surely his. Lo, the imperial will
In every feature! Mighty purpose lies
About the shut mouth, resolute and still.
Observe the head's pathetic attitude,
Bent forward, listening, — he that might not hear!
Ah, could the world's adoring gratitude,
So late to come, have made his life less drear!
Hearest thou, now, great soul beyond our ken,
Men's reverent voices answering thee, "Amen"?

MOZART

Most beautiful among the helpers thou!
All heaven's fresh air and sunshine at thy voice
Flood with refreshment many a weary brow,
And sad souls thrill with courage and rejoice
To hear God's gospel of pure gladness sound
So sure and clear in this bewildered world,
Till the sick vapors that our sense confound
By cheerful winds are into nothing whirled.
O matchless melody! perfect art!
lovely, lofty voice, unfaltering!
O strong and radiant and divine Mozart,
Among earth's benefactors crowned a king!
Loved shalt thou be while time may yet endure,
Spirit of health, sweet, sound, and wise, and pure.

SCHUBERT

At the open window I lean;
Flowers in the garden without
Faint in the heat and the drought;
What does the music mean?

For here, from the cold keys within,
Is a tempest of melody drawn;
Doubts, passionate questions, the dawn
Of high hope, and a triumph to win;

While out in the garden, blood-red
The poppy droops, faint in the heat
Of the noon, and the sea-wind so sweet
Caresses its delicate head.

And still the strong music goes on
With its storming of beautiful heights,
With its sorrow that heaven requites,
And the victory fought for is won!

High with thy gift didst thou reach,
Schubert, whose genius superb
Nothing could check or could curb:
Thou liftest the heart with thy speech!

CHOPIN

Calm is the close of the day,
All things are quiet and blest;
Low in the darkening west
The young moon sinks slowly away.

Without, in the twilight, I dream:
Within it is cheerful and bright
With faces that bloom in the light,
And the cold keys that silently gleam.

Then a magical touch draws near,
And a voice like a call of delight
Cleaves the calm of the beautiful night,
And I turn from my musing to hear.

Lo! the movement too wondrous to name!
Agitation and rapture, the press
As of myriad waves that caress,
And break into vanishing flame.

Ah! but the exquisite strain,
Sinking to pathos so sweet!
Is life then a lie and a cheat?
Hark to the hopeless refrain!

Comes a shock like the voice of a soul
Lost to good, to all beauty and joy,
Led alone by the powers that destroy,
And fighting with fiends for control.

Drops a chord like the grave's first clod.
Then again toss the waves of caprice,
"Wild, delicate, sweet, with no peace,
No health, and no yielding to God.

Siren, that charmest the air
With this potent and passionate spell,
Sad as songs of the angels that fell,
Thou leadest alone to despair!

What troubles the night? It grows chill —
Let the weird, wild music be;
Fronts us the infinite sea
And Nature is holy and still.

THE PIMPERNEL

She walks beside the silent shore,
The tide is high, the breeze is still;
No ripple breaks the ocean floor,
The sunshine sleeps upon the hill.

The turf is warm beneath her feet,
Bordering the beach of stone and shell,
And thick about her path the sweet
Red blossoms of the pimpernel.

"Oh, sleep not yet, my flower!" she cries,
"Nor prophesy of storm to come;
Tell me that under steadfast skies
Fair Winds shall bring my lover home."

She stoops to gather flower and shell,
She sits, and, smiling, studies each;
She hears the full tide rise and swell,

And whisper softly on the beach.

Waking, she dreams a golden dream,
Remembering with what still delight,
To watch the sunset's fading gleam,
Here by the waves they stood last night.

She leans on that encircling arm,
Divinely strong with power to draw
Her nature, as the moon doth charm
The swaying sea with heavenly law.

All lost in bliss the moments glide;
She feels his whisper, his caress;
The murmur of the mustering tide
Brings her no presage of distress.

What breaks her dream? She lifts her eyes
Reluctant to destroy the spell;
The color from her bright cheek dies, —
Close folded is the pimpernel.

With rapid glance she scans the sky;
Rises a sudden wind, and grows,
And charged with storm the cloud-heaps lie.
Well may the scarlet blossoms close!

A touch, and bliss is turned to bale!
Life only keeps the sense of pain;
The world holds naught save one white sail
Flying before the wind and rain.

Broken upon the wheel of fear
She wears the storm- vexed hour away;
And now in gold and fire draws near
The sunset of her troubled day.

But to her sky is yet denied
The sun that lights the world for her;
She sweeps the rose-flushed ocean wide
With eager eyes the quick tears blur;

And lonely, lonely all the space
Stretches, with never sign of sail,
And sadder grows her wistful face,
And all the sunset splendors fail.

And cold and pale, in still despair,

With heavier grief than tongue can tell,
She sinks, — upon her lips a prayer,
Her cheek against the pimpernel.

Bright blossoms wet with showery tears
On her shut eyes their droplets shed.
Only the wakened waves she hears,
That, singing, drown his rapid tread.

"Sweet, I am here!" Joy's gates swing wide,
And heaven is theirs, and all is well,
And left beside the ebbing tide,
Forgotten, is the pimpernel.

BY THE DEAD

O Poverty! till now I never knew
The meaning of the word! What lack is here!
O pale mask of a soul great, good, and true!
mocking semblance stretched upon a bier!

Each atom of this devastated face
Was so instinct with power, with warmth and light;
What desert is so desolate! No grace
Is left, no gleam, no change, no day, no night.

Where is the key that locked these gates of speech,
Once beautiful, where thought stood sentinel,
Where sweetness sat, where wisdom passed, to teach
Our weakness strength, our homage to compel?

Despoiled at last, and waste and barren lies
This once so rich domain. Where lives and moves,
In what new world, the splendor of these eyes
That dauntless lightened like imperial Jove's?

Annihilated, do you answer me?
Blown out and vanished like a candle flame?
Is nothing left but this pale effigy,
This silence drear, this dread without a name?

Has it been all in vain, our love and pride,
This yearning love that still pursues our friend
Into the awful dark, unsatisfied,
Bereft, and wrung with pain? Is this the end?

Would God so mock us? To our human sense
No answer reaches through the doubtful air;
Yet with a living hope, profound, intense,
Our tortured souls rebel against despair;

As bowing to the bitter fate we go
Drooping and dumb as if beneath a curse;
But does not pitying Heaven answer "No!"
With all the voices of the universe?

FOOTPRINTS IN THE SAND

Lazily, through the warm gray afternoon,
We sailed toward the land;
Over the long sweep of the billows, soon,
We saw on either hand
Peninsula and cape and silver beach
Unfold before our eyes,
Lighthouse and roof and spire and wooded reach
Grew clear beyond surmise.
Behind us lay the islands that we loved,
Touched by a wandering gleam,
Melting in distance, where the white sails moved
Softly as in a dream.
Drifting past buoy and scarlet beacon slow,
We gained the coast at last,
And up the harbor, where no wind did blow,
We drew, and anchor cast.
The lovely land! Green, the broad fields came down
Almost into the sea;
Nestled the quiet homesteads warm and brown,
Embraced by many a tree;
The gray above was streaked with smiling blue,
The snowy gulls sailed o'er;
The shining goldenrod waved, where it grew,
A welcome to the shore.
Peaceful the whole, and sweet. Beyond the sand
The dwelling-place I sought
Lay in the sunshine. All the scene I scanned,
Full of one wistful thought:
Saw any eyes our vessel near the shore
From vine-draped windows quaint?
Waited my bright, shy darling at the door,
Fairer than words could paint?
I did not see her gleaming golden head,
Nor hear her clear voice call;

As up the beach I went with rapid tread,
Lonely and still was all.
But on the smooth sand printed, far and near,
I saw her footsteps small;
Here had she loitered, here she hastened, here
She climbed the low stone wall.
Such pathos in those little footprints spoke,
I paused and lingered long;
Listening as far away the billows broke
With the old solemn song.
"The infinite hoary spray of the salt sea,"
In yet another tide,
Should wash away these traces utterly;
And in my heart I cried, —
"O thou Creator, when thy waves of Time,
The infinite hoary spray
That sweeps life from the earth at dawn and prime,
Have swept her soul away,
How shall I know it is not even as these
Light footprints in the sand,
That vanish into naught? For no man sees
Clearly what Thou hast planned."
And sadly musing, up the slope I pressed,
And sought her where she played,
By breeze and sunshine flattered and caressed,
A merry little maid.
And while I clasped her close and held her fast,
And looked into her face,
Half shy, half smiling, wholly glad at last
To rest in my embrace,
From the clear heaven of her innocent eyes
Leaped Love to answer me;
Divinely through the mortal shape that dies
Shone immortality!
What the winds hinted, what the awful sky
Held in its keeping, — all
The vast sea's prophesying suddenly
Grew clear as clarion call.
The secret nature strives to speak, yet hides,
Flashed from those human eyes
To slay my doubt: I felt that all the tides
Of death and change might rise
And devastate the world, yet I could see
This steady shining spark
Should live eternally, could never be
Lost in the unfathomed dark!
And when beneath a threatening sunset sky
We trimmed our sails and turned

Seaward again, with many a sweet good-by,
A quiet gladness burned
Within me, as I watched her tiny form
Go dancing up and down,
Light as a sandpiper before the storm,
Upon the beach-edge brown,
Waving her little kerchief to and fro
Till we were out of sight,
Sped by a wild wind that began to blow
Out of the troubled night;
And while we tossed upon an angry sea,
And round the lightning ran,
And muttering thunder rolled incessantly
As the black storm began,
I knew the fair and peaceful landscape lay
Safe hidden in the gloom,
Waiting the glad returning of the day
To smile again and bloom;
And sure as that to-morrow's sun would rise,
And day again would be,
Shone the sweet promise of those childish eyes
Wherein God answered me.

A BROKEN LILY

O Lily, dropped upon the gray sea-sand,
What time my fair love through the morning land
Led the rejoicing children, singing all
In happy chorus, to their festival,
Under green trees the flowery fields among;
Now, when the noon sun blazes o'er the sea,
And echo tells not of the song they sung,
And all thy silver splendor silently

Thou yieldest to the salt and bitter tide,
I find thee, and, remembering on whose breast
Thy day began in thy fresh beauty's pride,
Though of thy bloom and fragrance dispossessed,
Thou art to me than all June's flowers more sweet,
Fairer than Aphrodite's foam-kissed feet!

MAY MORNING

Warm, wild, rainy wind, blowing fitfully,

Stirring dreamy breakers on the slumberous May sea,
What shall fail to answer thee? What thing shall withstand
The spell of thine enchantment, flowing over sea and land?

All along the swamp-edge in the rain I go;
All about my head thou the loosened locks dost blow;
Like the German goose-girl in the fairy tale,
I watch across the shining pool my flock of ducks that sail.

Redly gleam the rose- haws, dripping with the wet,
Fruit of sober autumn, glowing crimson yet;
Slender swords of iris leaves cut the water clear,
And light green creeps the tender grass, thick spreading far and near.

Every last year's stalk is set with brown or golden studs;
All the boughs of bayberry are thick with scented buds;
Islanded in turfy velvet, where the ferns uncurl,
Lo! the large white duck's egg glimmers like a pearl!

Softly sing the billows, rushing, whispering low;
Freshly, oh! deliciously, the warm, wild wind doth blow!
Plaintive bleat of new- washed lambs comes faint from far away;
And clearly cry the little birds, alert and blithe and gay.

O happy, happy morning! O dear, familiar place!
O warm, sweet tears of Heaven, fast falling on my face!
well-remembered, rainy wind, blow all my care away,
That I may be a child again this blissful morn of May.

ALL'S WELL

What dost thou here, young wife, by the water-side,
Gathering crimson dulse?
Know'st thou not that the cloud in the west glooms wide,
And the wind has a hurrying pulse?

Peaceful the eastern waters before thee spread,
And the cliffs rise high behind,
While thou gatherest sea- weeds, green and brown and red,
To the coming trouble blind.

She lifts her eyes to the top of the granite crags,
And the color ebbs from her cheek,
Swift vapors skurry the black squall's tattered flags,
And she hears the gray gull shriek.

And like a blow is the thought of the little boat
By this on its homeward way,
A tiny skiff, like a cockle-shell afloat
In the tempest- threatened bay;

With husband and brother who sailed away to the town
When fair shone the morning sun,
To tarry but till the tide in the stream turned down,
Then seaward again to run.

Homeward she flies; the land-breeze strikes her cold;
A terror is in the sky;
Her little babe with his tumbled hair of gold
In her mother's arms doth lie.

She catches him up with a breathless, questioning cry:
"O mother, speak! Are they near? "
"Dear, almost home. At the western window high
Thy father watches in fear."

She climbs the stair: "O father, must they be lost?
He answers never a word;
Through the glass he watches the line the squall has crossed
As if no sound he heard.

And the Day of Doom seems come in the angry sky,
And a low roar fills the air;
In an awful stillness the dead-black waters lie,
And the rocks gleam ghastly and bare.

Is it a snow-white gull's wing fluttering there,
In the midst of that hush of dread?
Ah, no, 't is the narrow strip of canvas they dare
In the face of the storm to spread.

A moment more and all the furies are loose,
The coast line is blotted out,
The skiff is gone, the rain-cloud pours its sluice,
And she hears her father shout,

"Down with your sail! as if through the tumult wild,"
And the distance, his voice might reach;
And, stunned, she clasps still closer her rosy child,
Bereft of the power of speech.

But her heart cries low, as writhing it lies on the rack,
"Sweet, art thou fatherless?"
And swift to her mother she carries the little one back,

Where she waits in her sore distress.

Then into the heart of the storm she rushes forth;
Like leaden bullets the rain
Beats hard in her face, and the hurricane from the north
Would drive her back again.

It splits the shingles off the roof like a wedge,
It lashes her clothes and her hair,
But slowly she fights her way to the western ledge,
With the strength of her despair.

Through the flying spray, through the rain-cloud's shattered stream,
What shapes in the distance grope,
Like figures that haunt the shore of a dreadful dream?
She is wild with a desperate hope.

Have pity, merciful Heaven! Can it be?
Is it no vision that mocks?
From billow to billow the headlong plunging sea
Has tossed them high on the rocks;

And the hollow skiff like a child's toy lies on the ledge
This side of the roaring foam,
And up from the valley of death, from the grave's drear edge,
Like ghosts of men they come!

Oh sweetly, sweetly shines the sinking sun,
And the storm is swept away;
Piled high in the east are the cloud-heaps purple and dun,
And peacefully dies the day.

But a sweeter peace falls soft on the grateful souls
In the lonely isle that dwell,
And the whisper and rush of every wave that rolls
Seem murmuring, "All is well,"

THE SECRET

"Oh what saw you, gathering flowers so early this May morn?"
"I saw a shining blackbird loud whistling on a thorn;
I saw the mottled plover from the swamp-edge fly away;
I heard the blithe song-sparrows who welcomed the bright day;
I heard the curlew calling, oh, sweet, so sweet and far!
I saw the white gull twinkling in the blue sky like a star."
"And is the blackbird whistling yet, and does the curlew call,

And should I find your rapture if I saw and heard it all?
Life seems to me so hard to bear, perplexed with change and loss,
Heavy with pain, and weary still with care's perpetual cross,
Why should the white gull's twinkling wings, half lost amid the blue,
Bring any joy? Yet care and pain weigh just as much on you,
And you come back and look at me with such joy-beaming eyes
An angel might have been your guide through fields of Paradise!
"What is the secret Nature keeps to whisper in your ear
That sends the swift blood pulsing warm with such immortal cheer,
And makes your eyes shine like the morn, and rings sweet in your voice,
Like some clear, distant trumpet sound that bids the world rejoice?"
"Her secret? Nay, she speaks to me no word you might not hear.
Her voice is ever ready and her meaning ever clear:
But I love her with such passion that her lightest gesture seems
Divinely beautiful — she fills my life with golden dreams.
I tremble in her presence, to her every touch and tone;
I answer to her whisper — love has to worship grown.
She turns her solemn face to me, and lays within my hand
The key that puts her endless wealth for aye at my command;
And so, because I worship her, her benedictions rest
Upon me, and she folds me safe and warm upon her breast,
And in her sweet and awful eyes I gaze till I forget
The troubles that perplex our days, the tumult and the fret.
Oh, would you learn the word of power that lifts, all care above,
The sad soul up to Nature's heart? I answer, It is Love!"

SEASIDE GOLDENROD

Graceful, tossing plume of glowing gold,
Waving lonely on the rocky ledge;
Leaning seaward, lovely to behold,
Clinging to the high cliff's ragged edge;
Burning in the pure September sky,
Spike of gold against the stainless blue,
Do you watch the vessels drifting by?
Does the quiet day seem long to you?
Up to you I climb, perfect shape!
Poised so lightly 'twixt the sky and sea;
Looking out o'er headland, crag, and cape,
O'er the ocean's vague immensity.
Up to you my human thought I bring,
Sit me down your peaceful watch to share.
Do you hear the waves below us sing?
Feel you the soft fanning of the air?
How much of life's rapture is your right?
In earth's joy what may your portion be?

Rocked by breezes, touched by tender light,
Fed by dews and sung to by the sea!
Something of delight and of content
Must be yours, however vaguely known;
And your grace is mutely eloquent,
And your beauty makes the rock a throne.
Matters not to you, golden flower!
That such eyes of worship watch you sway;
But you make more sweet the dreamful hour
And you crown for me the tranquil day.

MARCH

The keen north wind pipes loud;
Swift scuds the flying cloud;
Light lies the new fallen snow;
The ice- clad eaves drip slow,
For glad Spring has begun,
And to the ardent sun
The earth, long time so bleak,
Turns a frost-bitten cheek.
Through the clear sky of March,
Blue to the topmost arch,
Swept by the New Year's gales,
The crow, harsh-clamoring, sails.
By the swift river's flood
The willow's golden blood
Mounts to the highest spray,
More vivid day by day;
And fast the maples now
Crimson through every bough,
And from the alder's crown
Swing the long catkins brown.
Gone is the winter's pain;
Though sorrow still remain,
Though eyes with tears be wet,
The voice of our regret
We hush, to hear the sweet
Far fall of summer's feet.
The Heavenly Father wise
Looks in the saddened eyes
Of our unworthiness,
Yet doth He cheer and bless.
Doubt and Despair are dead;
Hope dares to raise her head,
And whispers of delight

Fill the earth day and night.
The snowdrops by the door
Lift upward, sweet and pure,
Their delicate bells; and soon,
In the calm blaze of noon,
By lowly window-sills
Will laugh the daffodils!

SONG

The clover blossoms kiss her feet,
She is so sweet,
While I, who may not kiss her hand,
Bless all the wild flowers in the land.

Soft sunshine falls across her breast,
She is so blest.
I 'm jealous of its arms of gold,
Oh that these arms her form might fold!
Gently the breezes kiss her hair,

She is so fair.
Let flowers and sun and breeze go by,
O dearest! Love me or I die.

Oscar Laighton

THE WHITE ROVER

They called the little schooner the White Rover,
When they lightly launched her on the brimming tide;
Stanch and trim she was to sail the broad seas over,
And with cheers they spread her snowy canvas wide;

And a thing of beauty, forth she fared to wrestle
With the. wild, uncertain ocean, far and near,
And no evil thing befell the graceful vessel,
And she sailed in storm and sunshine many a year.

But at last a rumor grew that she was haunted;
That up her slender masts her sails had flown
Unhelped by human hands, as if enchanted,
As she rocked upon her moorings all alone.

Howe'er that be, one day in winter weather,
When the bitter north was raging at its worst,
And wind and cold vexed the roused sea together,
Till Dante's frozen hell seemed less accurst,

Two fishermen, to draw their trawls essaying,
Seized by the hurricane that ploughed the bay,
Were swept across the waste; and hardly weighing
Death's chance, the Rover reefed and bore away

To save them, — reached them, shuddering where they waited
Their quick destruction, tossing white and dumb,
And caught them from perdition; then, belated,
Strove to return the rough way she had come.

But there was no returning! Fierce as lightning
The eager cold grew keener, more intense.
Across her homeward track the billows, whitening,
In crested mountains rolling, drove her thence;

Till her brave crew, benumbed, gave up the battle,
Clad in a mail of ice that weighed like lead;
They heard the crusted blocks and rigging rattle,
They saw the sails like sheets of iron spread.

And powerless before the gale they drifted,
Till swiftly dropped the black and hopeless night.
The wild tornado never lulled nor shifted,
But drove them toward the coast upon their right,

And flung the frozen schooner, all sail standing,
Stiff as an iceberg on the icy shore;
And half alive, her torpid people, landing,
Crept to the lighthouse, and were safe once more.

Then what befell the vessel, standing solemn
Through that tremendous night of cold and storm,
Upon the frost-locked land, a frigid column,
Beneath the stars, a silent, glittering form!

None ever saw her more! The tide upbore her,
Released her fastened keel, and ere the day,
Without a guide, and all the world before her,
The sad, forsaken Rover sailed away.

But sometimes, when in summer twilight blending
Sunset and moonrise mingle their rich light,
Or when on noonday mists the sun is spending

His glory, till they glimmer thin and white,

Upon the dim horizon melting, gleaming,
Slender, ethereal, like a lovely ghost
Soft looming, in the hazy distance dreaming,
Or gliding like a film along the coast,

I seem to see her yet: and skippers hoary,
Sailors and fishermen, will still relate
Among their sea- worn mates the simple story
Of how the wandering Rover met her fate;

And shake their heads: "Perhaps the tempest wrecked her,
But snug and trim and tidy, fore and aft,
I 've seen the vessel since, or else her spectre,
Sailing as never yet sailed earthly craft,

Straight in the wind's teeth; and with steady motion
Cleaving a calm as if it blew a gale!"
And they are sure her wraith still haunts the ocean,
Mocking the sight with semblance of a sail.

CONTRAST

The day is bitter. Through the hollow sky
Rolls the clear sun, inexorably bright,
Glares on the shrinking earth, a lidless eye,
Shedding no warmth, but floods of blinding light.

The hurricane roars loud. The facile sea
With passionate resentment writhes and raves
Beneath its maddening whip, and furiously
Responds with all the thunder of its waves.

The iron rock, ice-locked, snow-sheathed, lies still,
The centre of this devastated world,
Beaten and lashed by wind and sea at will,
Buried in spray by the fierce breakers hurled.

Cold, raging desolation! Out of it,
Swift-footed, eager, noiseless as the light,
Glides my adventurous thought, and lo, I sit
With Memnon and the desert in my sight.

Silence and breathless heat! A torrid land,
Unbroken to the vast horizon's verge,

Save once, where from the waste of level sand
All motionless the clustered palms emerge.

Hot the wide earth and hot the blazing sky,
And still as death, unchanged since time began.
Far in the shimmering distance silently
Creeps like a snake the lessening caravan.

And on the great lips of the statue old
Broods silence, and no zephyr stirs the palm.
Nature forgets her tempests and her cold,
And breathes in peace. "There is no joy but calm."

A FADED GLOVE

My little granddaughter, who fain would know
Why, folded close in scented satin fine,
I keep a relic faded long ago,
This pearl-gray, dainty, withered glove of. mine,

Listen: I'll tell you. It is fifty years
Since the fair day I laid my treasure here.
But yesterday to me the time appears;
Ages ago to you, I know, my dear.

Upon this palm, now withered as my cheek,
Love laid his first kiss, doubting and afraid:
Oh, swift and strong across me while I speak
Comes memory of Love's might, my little maid!

I yet was so unconscious! 'Twas a night —
Some festal night; my sisters were above,
Not ready quite; but I, cloaked all in white,
Waited "below, and, fastening my glove,

Looked up with smiling speech to him who stood
Observing me, so still and so intent,
I wondered somewhat at his quiet mood,
Till it flashed on me what the silence meant.

What sudden fire of dawn my sky o'erspread!
What low melodious thunder broke my calm!
Could I be dreaming that this glorious head
Was bending low above my girlish palm?

His majesty of mien proclaimed him king;

His lowly gesture said, "I am your slave; "
Beneath my feet the firm earth seemed to swing,
Unstable as storm-driven wind and wave.

Ah, beautiful and terrible and sweet
The matchless moment! Was it life or death,
Or day or night? For my heart ceased to beat,
And heaven and earth changed in a single breath.

And, like a harp some hand of power doth smite
To sudden harmony, my soul awoke,
And, answering, rose to match his spirit's height,
While not a word the mystic silence broke.

'T was but an instant. Down the echoing stair
Swept voices, laughter, wafts of melody, —
My sisters three, in draperies light as air;
But like a dream the whole world seemed to me,

As, steadying my whirling thoughts, I strove
To grasp a truth so wondrous, so divine.
I shut this hand, this little tinted glove,
To keep its secret mine, and only mine.

And like an empty show the brilliant hours
Passed by, with beauty, music, pleasure thronged,
Phantasmagoria of light and flowers;
But only one delight to me belonged,

One thought, one wish, one hope, one joy, one fear,
One dizzy rapture, one star in the sky, —
The solemn sky that bent to bring God near:
I would have been content that night to die.

Only a touch upon this little glove,
And, lo, the lofty marvel which it wrought!
You wonder; for as yet you know not love,
Oh, sweet my child, my lily yet unsought!

The glove is faded, but immortal joy
Lives in the kiss; its memory cannot fade;
And when Death's clasp this pale hand shall destroy,
The sacred glove shall in my grave be laid.

PORTENT

When the darkness drew away at the dawning of the day,
I heard the medricks screaming loud and shrill across the hay;
And I wondered to "behold all the sky in ruddy gold,
Flashing into fire and flame where the clouds like billows rolled.

Red the sea ran east and west, burning broke each tumbling crest,
Where the waves, like shattered rubies, leaped and fell and could not rest;
Every rock was carmine-flushed, every sail like roses blushed,
Flying swift before the wind from the south that roared and rushed.

"Is it judgment day?" I said, gazing out o'er billows red,
Gazing up at crimson vapors, crowding, drifting overhead,
Listening to the great uproar of the waters on the shore,
To the wild sad-crying sea-birds, buffeted and beaten sore.

"Is the end of time at hand? is this pageant, strange and grand,
A portent of destruction blazing fierce o'er sea and land?"
Then the scarlet ebbed, and slow, sky above and earth below,
Drowned in melancholy purple, seemed with grief to overflow.

And while thus I gazed, the day, growing stronger, turned to gray;
All the transitory splendor and the beauty passed away;
And I recognized the sign of the color poured like wine
In this morn of late October as from clusters of the vine.

'Twas the ripeness of the year; soon, I knew, must disappear
All the warmth and light and happiness that made the time so dear;
And again our souls must wait while the bare earth, desolate,
Bore in patience and in silence all the winter's wrath and hate.

SONG

Sing, little bird, oh sing!
How sweet thy voice and clear!
How fine the airy measures ring,
The sad old world to cheer!

Bloom, little flower, oh bloom!
Thou makest glad the day;
A scented torch, thou dost illume
The darkness of the way,

Dance, little child, oh dance!
While sweet the small birds sing,
And flowers bloom fair, and every glance
Of sunshine tells of spring.

Oh! bloom, and sing, and smile,
Child, bird, and flower, and make
The sad old world forget awhile
Its sorrow for your sake!

RENUNCIATION

Like scattered flowers blown all about the bay,
The rosy sails, lit with the sunrise, shine;
The white stars in the brightness fade away;
In perfect silence dawns the day divine.

"Oh bring me neither gifts of good or ill,
Delicious day! Let only peace be mine!"
And the fair hours, advancing calm and still,
Passed by her mute, nor brought her word or sign.

But when the glory of the sunset flame
Held all the world in triumph brief and sweet,
The last bright hour, with faltering footsteps, came
And laid a gift august before her feet.

Yet she entreated, "Peace! Take back your gift,
O golden hour! I am content to be
Lonely as yonder fading sails that drift
'Neath saddened skies upon the silent sea."

Fate answered her, "The gods may not recall
Their gifts, once given. Be wise, therefore. Accept
Their bounty gratefully; for not to all
Such largess falls. " She bowed her head and wept.

She turned her from the sunset's red and gold,
She faced the dim East's waning violet,
She saw the twilight stealing pale and cold,
And all her soul was wrung with her regret.

Pure, powerful, triumphant music shook
The listening air and floated up the sky;
The dust and ashes of her life she took
And passed the gift of splendid beauty by.

"But oh, must storm and strife be mine," she cried,
"Forever? Shall I never find repose?
Mocked by mirage of hope and still defied

And buffeted by every wind that blows!"

From farthest distance high a clear voice rang,
"Ashes and dust shall blossom like the rose!
Climb thou above the tempests," sweet it sang;
"Patience! ' On every height there lies repose.'

SONG

Oh the fragrance of the air
With the breathing of the flowers!
Oh the isles of cloudlets fair,
Shining after balmy showers!

Oh the freshly rippling notes!
Oh the warbling, loud and long,
From a thousand golden throats!
Oh the south wind's tender song!

Oh the mellow dip of oars
Through the dreamy afternoon!
Oh the waves that clasp the shores,
Chanting one delicious tune!

Wears the warm, enchanted day
To the last of its rich hours,
While my heart, in the sweet May,
Buds and blossoms with the flowers.

TWO SONNETS

Not so! You stand as long ago a king
Stood on the seashore, bidding back the tide
That onward rolled resistless still, to fling
Its awful volume landward, wild and wide.
And just as impotent is your command
To stem the tide that rises in my soul.
It ebbs not at the lifting of your hand,
It owns no curb, it yields to no control;
Mighty it is, and of the elements, —
Brother of winds and lightning, cold and fire,
Subtle as light, as steadfast and intense;
Sweet as the music of Apollo's lyre.
You think to rule the ocean's ebb and flow

With that soft woman's hand? Nay, love, not so.

And like the lighthouse on the rock you stand,
And pierce the distance with your searching eyes;
Nor do you heed the waves that storm the land
And endlessly about you fall and rise,
But seek the ships that wander night and day
Within the dim horizon's shadowy ring;
And some with flashing glance you warn away,
And some you beckon with sweet welcoming.
So steadfast still you keep your lofty place,
Safe from the tumult of the restless tide,
Firm as the rock in your resisting grace,
And strong through humble duty, not through pride.
While I — I cast my life before your feet,
And only live that I may love you, sweet!

DAYBREAK

In the morning twilight, while the household yet
Slumbering securely day and night forget,
Lightly o'er the threshold I pass, and breathless stand
In the dream of beauty that rests on sea and land.

Fresh and calm and dewy, bathed in delicate air,
The happy earth awakens and grows of day aware.
Sweetly breaks the silence some bird's delicious trill,
And from the southern distance a breeze begins to thrill.

All the stars have faded, and the low large moon
O'er the western water will have vanished soon.
Crystal-clear and cloudless the awful arch is bright,
As up the conscious heaven streams the growing light.

On the far horizon softly sleeps the haze;
O'er the ocean spaces steal the rosy rays;
Winds and waves are quiet, only far away
'Gainst the rock a breaker tosses sudden spray.

Out behind the headland glides the coaster slow,
All her canvas blushing in the ruddy glow;
Where the steadfast lighthouse watches day and night,
Beautiful and stately she passes out of sight.

Day that risest splendid, with promise so divine,
Mine is thy perfect gladness, thy loveliness is mine.

Thou touchest with thy blessing God's creatures great and small;
None shalt thou find more grateful than I among them all.

I turn my face in worship to the glory of the East.
I thank the lavish giver of my life's perpetual feast,
And fain would I be worthy to partake of Nature's bliss,
And share with her a moment so exquisite as this!

SONG

Love, Love, Love!
Whether it rain or shine,
Whether the clouds frown or the sky is clear
Whether the thunder fill the air with fear,
Whether the winter rage or peace is here,
If only thou art near,
Then are all days divine.

O Love, Love, Love!
Where thou art not, the place
Is sad to me as death. It would be cold
In heaven without thee, if I might not hold
Thy hand in mine, if I might not behold
The beauty manifold,
The wonder of thy face.

THE NESTLING SWALLOWS

The summer day was spoiled with fitful storm;
At night the wind died, and the soft rain dropped
With lulling murmur, and the air was warm,
And all the tumult and the trouble stopped.

We sat within the bright and quiet room,
Glowing with light and flowers and friendliness;
And faces in the radiance seemed to bloom,
Touched into beauty as by a caress.

And one struck music from the ivory keys, —
Beethoven's music; and the awful chords
Upbore us like the waves of mighty seas
That sing aloud, "All glory is the Lord's! "

And the great sound awoke beneath the eaves

The nestling swallows; and their twittering cry,
With the light touch of raindrops on the leaves,
Broke into the grand surging melody.

Across its deep, tremendous questioning,
Its solemn acquiescence, low and clear,
The rippling notes ran sweet, with airy ring
Surprised, inquiring, but devoid of fear;

Lapsing to silence at the music's close,
A dreamy clamor, a contented stir.
"It made no discord," smiling, as he rose,
Said the great master's great interpreter.

No discord, truly! Ever Nature weaves
Her sunshine with her shadow, joy with pain:
The asking thunder through high heaven that cleaves
Is lost in the low ripple of the rain.

About the edges of the dread abyss
The innocent blossoms laugh toward the sun;
Questions of life and death, of bale or bliss,
A thousand tender touches overrun.

Why should I chronicle so slight a thing?
But such things light up life like wayside flowers,
And memory, like a bird with folded wing,
Broods with still joy o'er such delicious hours.

Dear unforgotten time! Fair summer night!
Thy nestling swallows and thy dropping rain,
The golden music and the faces bright,
Will steal with constant sweetness back again.

A joy to keep when winter darkness comes;
A living sense of beauty to recall;
A warm, bright thought, when bitter cold benumbs,
To make me glad and grateful. That is all.

VESPER SONG

Lies the sunset splendor far and wide,
On the golden tide!
Drifting slow toward yonder evening red,
With the faint stars sparkling overhead,
Peacefully we glide.

Sweet is rest: the summer day is done,
Gone the ardent sun.
All is still: no wind of twilight blows;
Shuts the evening like a crimson rose;
Night comes like a nun.

Lift we loving voices, pure and clear,
To the Father's ear;
Fragrant as the flowers the thoughts we raise
Up to heaven, while o'er the ocean ways
Draws the darkness near.

FLOWERS IN OCTOBER

The long black ledges are white with gulls,
As if the breakers had left their foam;
With the dying daylight the wild wind lulls,
And the scattered fishing-boats steer for home.

On the crag I sit, with the east before.
The sun behind me is low in the sky;
Warm is its touch on the rocky shore;
Sad the vast ocean spaces lie.

The cricket is hoarse in the faded grass;
The low bush rustles so thin and sere;
Swift overhead the small birds pass,
With cries that are lonely and sweet and clear.

The last chill asters their petals fold
And gone is the morning-glory's bell,
But close in a loving hand I hold
Long sprays of the scarlet pimpernel,

And thick at my feet are blossom and leaf,
Blossoms rich red as the robes of kings;
Hardly they 're touched by the autumn's grief;
Do they surmise what the winter brings?

I turn my eyes from the sweet, sad sky,
From the foam-white gulls and the sails that gleam,
To muse on the scattered flowers that lie
Lost as yet in a summer dream.

O darlings, nursed by the salt sea- spray!

O shapes of beauty so quaint and bright!
But for a little the frosts delay,
Soon will be ended your brief delight.

Could I but succor you, every one,
Spread wings of safety 'twixt harm and you;
Call from its southern travel the sun,
Banish the snow from the arching blue!

It may not be, and the frosts must fall,
The winter must reign in the summer's stead;
But, though you perish beyond recall,
Ever I love you, alive or dead.

WAIT

Are the roses fallen, dear my child?
Has the winter left us only thorns,
Sharp and shuddering stalks in tangles wild,
Set with cruel teeth and iron horns?

Wait a little, fret not, and at last
Beauty will the barren boughs again
Tenderly re-clothe, when snows are past,
And the earth grows glad in sun and rain.

Never vex your heart nor tear your hands,
Searching 'mid the thorns for vanished bliss;
For the soul that patience understands
Needs no wisdom more divine than this:

Wait! The sweet flowers of the coming spring
Beautiful as those you mourn shall be.
Wait! for happy birds are sure to sing,
While new roses bloom for you and me.

KAREN

At her low quaint wheel she sits to spin,
Deftly drawing the long, light rolls
Of carded wool through her fingers thin,
By the fireside at the Isles of Shoals.

She is not pretty, she is not young,

Poor homesick Karen, who sits and spins,
Humming a song in her native tongue,
That falters and stops, and again begins,

While her wheel flies fast, with its drowsy hum,
And she makes a picture of pensive grace
As thoughts of her well-loved Norway come
And deepen the shadows across her face.

Her collar is white as the drifted snow,
And she spun and wove her blue gown fine
With those busy hands. See, a flitting glow
Makes her pale cheek burn and her dark eyes shine!

Left you a lover in that far land,
Karen sad, that you pine so long?
Would I could unravel and understand
That sorrowful, sweet Norwegian song!

When the spring wind blew, the "America wind,"
As your people call it, that bears away
Their youths and maidens a home to find
In this distant country, could you not stay

And live in that dear Norway still,
And let the emigrant crowd sail West
Without you? Well, you have had your will.
Why would you fly from your sheltering nest?

O homesick Karen, listen to me:
You are not young, and you are not fair,
But Waldemar no one else can see,
For he carries your image everywhere.

Is he too boyish a lover for you,
With all his soul in his frank blue eyes?
Feign you unconsciousness? Is it true
You know not his heart in your calm hand lies?

Handsome and gentle and good is he;
Loves you, Karen, better than life;
Do but consider him, can't you see
What a happy woman would be his wife?

You won't be merry? You can't be glad?
Still must you mourn for that home afar?
"Well, here is an end of a hope I had.
And I am sorry for Waldemar!

A MUSSEL SHELL

Why art thou colored like the evening sky
Sorrowing for sunset? Lovely dost thou lie,
Bared by the washing of the eager brine,
At the snow's motionless and wind-carved line.

Cold stretch the snows, cold throng the waves, the wind
Stings sharp, — an icy fire, a touch unkind, —
And sighs as if with passion of regret,
The while I mark thy tints of violet.

O beauty strange! shape of perfect grace,
Whereon the lovely waves of color trace
The history of the years that passed thee by,
And touched thee with the pathos of the sky!

The sea shall crush thee; yea, the ponderous wave
Up the loose beach shall grind, and scoop thy grave,
Thou thought of God! What more than thou am I?
Both transient as the sad wind's passing sigh.

TRUST

See how the wind is hauling point by point to the south,
By the boats in the little harbor, that swing to its lightest touch;
And the coasting craft emerge from the far-off river's mouth,
And on the rocks the breakers relax their impotent clutch.

At last is the tempest ended, the bitter northeast appeased,
And the world will soon be sparkling in clear white fire and dew,
And the sullen clouds melt swiftly, by the might of warm wind seized,
And the heavens shine in splendor, where broadens the matchless blue.

Carol the birds in chorus; glitters the snow-white gull,
Screaming loud in mid-air, slow-soaring high with delight;
And the rosebuds loosen their petals, the drenched flowers, sodden and dull,
Break out into stars of purple and gold and crimson and white.

Where wert thou, Spirit of Beauty, while earth lay cold and dark,
And the chill wind struck to our hearts, and the sky like an enemy scowled,
And we crept through the mists desponding, and never a glimmering spark

Shot a ray through the gloom while the storm like a demon groveled and growled?

Where art thou, Heavenly Father, when thy world seems spoiled with sin,
And darker far than thy tempest arises the smoke of doubt,
That blackens the sky of the soul? — for faith is hard to win:
To our finite sight wrong triumphs and noble things die out,

While shapes of monstrous evil make fearful thy nights and days,
And murder stalks unhindered, working its hideous will,
And innocence, gentleness, charity seem to forsake earth's ways,
And in the hearts of thy creatures are madness and nameless ill.

Behind the cloud Thou waitest, hidden, yet very near,
Infinite Spirit of Beauty, Infinite Power of Good!
At last Thou wilt scatter the vapors, and all things shall be clear,
And evil shall vanish away like a mist by the wind pursued.

MODJESKA

Deft hands called Chopin's music from the keys.
Silent she sat, her slender figure's poise
Flower-like and fine and full of lofty ease;
She heard her Poland's most consummate voice
From power to pathos falter, sink and change;
The music of her land, the wondrous high,
Utmost expression of its genius strange, —
Incarnate sadness breathed in melody.
Silent and thrilled she sat, her lovely face
Flushing and paling like a delicate rose
Shaken by summer winds from its repose
Softly this way and that with tender grace,
Now touched by sun, now into shadow turned, —
While bright with kindred fire her deep eyes burned!

SONG

O swallow, sailing lightly
The crystal deeps of blue,
With flashing wings that brightly
Glitter the sunshine through,

What sayest thou, returning
From sunny lands and fair,
That summer roses burning

Shall light the fragrant air?

That merry days thou bringest,
And gone is winter's woe, —
Is this the song thou singest?
Gay prophet, is it so?

I know all beauties follow
Swift in thy shining track,
But to my heart, swallow,
Canst thou bring summer back?

No shaft of sunshine glorious
Shall melt my winter snows,
No kiss of June victorious
Awake for me the rose!

LARS

"Tell us a story of these isles," they said,
The daughters of the West, whose eyes had seen
For the first time the circling sea, instead
Of the blown prairie's waves of grassy green:

"Tell us of wreck and peril, storm and cold,
Wild as the wildest." Under summer stars,
With the slow moonrise at our back, I told
The story of the young Norwegian, Lars.

That youth with the black eyebrows sharply drawn
In strong curves, like some sea-bird's wings out-spread
O'er his dark eyes, is Lars, and this fair dawn
Of womanhood, the maiden he will wed.

She loves him for the dangers he has past.
Her rosy beauty glowed before his stern
And vigilant regard, until at last
Her sweetness vanquished Lars the taciturn.

For he is ever quiet, strong, and wise;
Wastes nothing, not a gesture nor a breath;
Forgets not, gazing in the maiden's eyes,
A year ago it was not love, but death,

That clasped him, and can hardly learn as yet
How to be merry, haunted by that pain

And terror, and remembering with regret
The comrade he can never see again.

Out from the harbor on that winter day
Sailed the two men to set their trawl together.
Down swept the sudden snow-squall o'er the bay,
And hurled their slight boat onward like a feather.

They tossed they knew not whither, till at last
Under the lighthouse cliff they found a lee,
And out the road-lines of the trawl they cast
To moor her, if so happy they might be.

But quick the slender road-lines snapt in twain
In the wild breakers, and once more they tossed
Adrift; and, watching from his misty pane,
The lighthouse keeper muttered, "They are lost!"

Lifted the snow: night fell; swift cleared the sky;
The air grew sharp as death with polar cold;
Raged the insensate gale, and flashing high
In starlight keen the hissing billows rolled.

Driven before the wind's incessant scourge
All night they fled, — one dead ere morning lay.
Lars saw his strange, drawn countenance emerge
In the fierce sunrise light of that drear day,

And thought, "A little space and I shall be
Even as he," and, gazing in despair
O'er the wide, weltering waste, no sign could see
Of hope, or help, or comfort, anywhere.

Two hundred miles before the hurricane
The dead and living drove across the sea.
The third day dawned. His dim eyes saw again
The vast green plain, breaking eternally

In ghastly waves. But in the early light,
On the horizon glittering like a star,
Fast growing, looming tall, with canvas white,
Sailed his salvation southward from afar!

Down she bore, rushing o'er the hills of brine,
Straight for his feeble signal. As she past,
Out from the schooner's deck they flung a line,
And o'er his head the open noose was cast.

Clutching with both his hands the bowline knot
Caught at his throat, swift drawn through fire he seemed,
Whelmed in the icy sea, and he forgot
Life, death, and all things, — yet he thought he dreamed

A dread voice cried, "We 've lost him!" and a sting
Of anguish pierced his clouded senses through;
A moment more, and like a lifeless thing
He lay among the eager, pitying crew.

Long time he swooned, while o'er the ocean vast
The dead man tossed alone, they knew not where;
But youth and health triumphant were at last,
And here is Lars, you see, and here the fair

Young snow-and-rose-bloom maiden he will wed.
His face is kindly, though it seems so stern.
Death passed him by, and life begins instead,
For Thora sweet and Lars the taciturn.

SONG

A rushing of wings in the dawn,
A flight of birds in the sky!
The darkness of night withdrawn,
In an outburst of melody!

O birds through the heaven that soar
With such tumult of jubilant song!
The shadows are flying before,
For the rapture of life is strong,

And my spirit leaps to the light
On the wings of its hope new-born,
And I follow your radiant flight
Through the golden halls of morn!

A MEMORABLE MURDER. A TRUE STORY.

At the Isles of Shoals, on the 5th of March in the year 1873, occurred one of the most monstrous tragedies ever enacted on this planet. The sickening details of the double murder are well known; the newspapers teemed with them for months: but the pathos of the story is not realized; the world does not know how gentle a life these poor people led, how innocently happy were their quiet days. They were all Norwegians. The more I see of the natives of this far-off land, the more I admire the fine qualities which seem to characterize them as a race. Gentle, faithful, intelligent, God-fearing human beings, they daily use such courtesy toward each other and all who come in contact with them, as puts our ruder Yankee manners to shame. The men and women living on this lonely island were like the sweet, honest, simple folk we read of in Bjornson's charming Norwegian stories, full of kindly thoughts and ways. The murdered Anethe might have been the Eli of Bjornson's beautiful Arne or the Ragnhild of Boyesen's lovely romance. They rejoiced to find a home just such as they desired in this peaceful place; the women took such pleasure in the little house which they kept so neat and bright, in their flock of hens, their little dog Ringe, and all their humble belongings! The Norwegians are an exceptionally affectionate people; family ties are very strong and precious among them. Let me tell the story of their sorrow as simply as may be.

Louis Wagner murdered Anethe and Karen Christensen at midnight on the 5th of March, two years ago this spring. The whole affair shows the calmness of a practiced hand; there was no malice in the deed, no heat; it was one of the coolest instances of deliberation ever chronicled in the annals of crime. He admits that these people had shown him nothing but kindness. He says in so many words, "They were my best friends." They looked upon him as a brother. Yet he did not hesitate to murder them. The island called Smutty-Nose by human perversity (since in old times it bore the pleasanter title of Haley's Island) was selected to be the scene of this disaster. Long ago I lived two years upon it, and know well its whitened ledges and grassy slopes, its low thickets of wild-rose and bayberry, its sea-wall still intact, connecting it with the small island Malaga, opposite Appledore, and the ruined break-water which links it with Cedar Island on the other side. A lonely cairn, erected by some long ago forgotten fishermen or sailors, stands upon the highest rock at the southeastern extremity; at its western end a few houses are scattered, small, rude dwellings, with the square old Haley house near; two or three fish-houses are falling into decay about the water-side, and the ancient wharf drops stone by stone into the little cove, where every day the tide ebbs and flows and ebbs again with pleasant sound and freshness. Near the houses is a small grave-yard, where a few of the natives sleep, and not far, the graves of the fourteen Spaniards lost in the wreck of the ship Sagunto in the year 1813. I used to think it was a pleasant place, that low, rocky, and grassy island, though so wild and lonely.

From the little town of Laurvig, near Christiania, in Norway, came John and Maren Hontvet to this country, and five years ago took up their abode in this desolate spot, in one of the cottages facing the cove and Appledore. And there they lived through the long winters and the lovely summers, John making a comfortable living by fishing, Maren, his wife, keeping as bright and tidy and sweet a little home for him as man could desire. The bit of garden they cultivated in the summer was a pleasure to them; they made their house as pretty as they could with paint and paper and gay pictures, and Maren had a shelf for her plants at the window; and John was always so good to her, so kind and thoughtful of her comfort and of what would please her, she was entirely happy. Sometimes she was a little lonely, perhaps, when he was tossing afar off on the sea, setting or hauling his trawls, or had sailed to Portsmouth to sell his fish. So that she was doubly glad when the news came that some of her people were coming over from Norway to live with her. And first, in the month of May, 1871, came her sister Karen, who stayed only a short time with Maren, and then came to Appledore, where she lived at service two years, till within a fortnight of her death. The first time I saw Maren, she brought her sister to us, and I was charmed with the little woman's beautiful behavior; she was so gentle, courteous, decorous, she left on my mind a most delightful impression. Her face struck me as remarkably good and intelligent, and her gray eyes were full of light.

Karen was a rather sad-looking woman, about twenty-nine years old; she had lost a lover in Norway long since, and in her heart she fretted and mourned for this continually: she could not speak a word of

English at first, but went patiently about her work and soon learned enough, and proved herself an excellent servant, doing faithfully and thoroughly everything she under took, as is the way of her people generally. Her personal neatness was most attractive. She wore gowns made of cloth woven by herself in Norway, a coarse blue stuff, always neat and clean, and often I used to watch her as she sat by the fire spinning at a spinning-wheel brought from her own country; she made such a pretty picture, with her blue gown and fresh white apron, and the nice, clear white muslin bow with which she was in the habit of fastening her linen collar, that she was very agreeable to look upon. She had a pensive way of letting her head droop a little sideways as she spun, and while the low wheel hummed monotonously, she would sit crooning sweet, sad old Norwegian airs by the hour together, perfectly unconscious that she was affording such pleasure to a pair of appreciative eyes. On the 12th of October, 1872, in the second year of her stay with us, her brother, Ivan Christensen, and his wife, Anethe Mathea, came over from their Norseland in an evil day, and joined Maren and John at their island, living in the same house with them.

Ivan and Anethe had been married only since Christmas of the preceding year. Ivan was tall, light haired, rather quiet and grave. Anethe was young, fair, and merry, with thick, bright sunny hair, which was so long it reached, when unbraided, nearly to her knees; blue-eyed, with brilliant teeth and clear, fresh complexion, beautiful, and beloved beyond expression by her young husband, Ivan. Mathew Hontvet, John's brother, had also joined the little circle a year before, and now Maren's happiness was complete. Delighted to welcome them all, she made all things pleasant for them, and she told me only a few days ago, "I never was so happy in my life as when we were all living there together." So they abode in peace and quiet, with not an evil thought in their minds, kind and considerate toward each other, the men devoted to their women and the women repaying them with interest, till out of the perfectly cloudless sky one day a blot descended, without a whisper of warning, and brought ruin and desolation into that peaceful home.

Louis Wagner, who had been in this country seven years, appeared at the Shoals two years before the date of the murder. He lived about the islands during that time. He was born in Ueckermunde, a small town of lower Pomeranie, in Northern Prussia. Very little is known about him, though there were vague rumors that his past life had not been without difficulties, and he had boasted foolishly among his mates that "not many had done what he had done and got off in safety;" but people did not trouble themselves about him or his past, all having enough to do to earn their bread and keep the wolf from the door. Maren describes him as tall, powerful, dark, with a peculiarly quiet manner. She says she never saw him drunk—he seemed always anxious to keep his wits about him: he would linger on the outskirts of a drunken brawl, listening to and absorbing everything, but never mixing himself up in any disturbance. He was always lurking in corners, lingering, looking, listening, and he would look no man straight in the eyes. She spoke, however, of having once heard him disputing with some sailors, at table, about some point of navigation; she did not understand it, but all were against Louis, and, waxing warm, all strove to show him he was in the wrong. As he rose and left the table she heard him mutter to himself with an oath, "I know I'm wrong, but I'll never give in!" During the winter preceding the one in which his hideous deed was committed, he lived at Star Island and fished alone, in a wherry; but he made very little money, and came often over to the Hontvets, where Maren gave him food when he was suffering from want, and where he received always a welcome and the utmost kindness. In the following June he joined Hontvet in his business of fishing, and took up his abode as one of the family at Smutty-Nose. During the summer he was "crippled," as he said, by the rheumatism, and they were all very good to him, and sheltered, fed, nursed, and waited upon him the greater part of the season. He remained with them five weeks after Ivan and Anethe arrived, so that he grew to know Anethe as well as Maren, and was looked upon as a brother by all of them, as I have said before. Nothing occurred to show his true character, and in November he left the island and the kind people whose hospitality he was to repay so fearfully, and going to Portsmouth he took passage in another fishing schooner, the Addison Gilbert, which was presently wrecked off the coast, and he was again thrown out of employment. Very recklessly he said to Waldemar Ingebertsen, to Charles Jonsen, and even to John Hontvet himself, at different times, that "he must have money if he murdered for it." He loafed about Portsmouth eight weeks, doing nothing. Meanwhile Karen left our service in February, intending to go to Boston and work at a sewing machine, for she was not strong and thought she should like it better than housework, but before going she lingered awhile with her sister Maren-fatal delay for her! Maren told me that during this time Karen went to Portsmouth and had her teeth removed, meaning to provide herself with a new set. At the Jonsens', where Louis was staying, one day she spoke to Mrs. Jonsen of her mouth, that it was so sensitive since the teeth had been taken out; and Mrs. Jonsen asked her how long she must wait before the new set could be put in. Karen replied that it would be three months. Louis Wagner was walking up and down at the other end of the room with his arms folded, his favorite attitude. Mrs. Jonsen's daughter passed near him and heard him mutter, "Three months! What is the use! In three months you will be dead!" He did not know the girl was so near, and turning, he confronted her. He knew she must have heard what he said, and he glared at her like a wild man.

On the fifth day of March, 1873, John Hontvet, his brother Mathew, and Ivan Christensen set sail in John's little schooner, the Clara Bella, to draw their trawls. At that time four of the islands were inhabited: one family on White Island, at the light-house; the workmen who were building the new hotel on Star Island, and one or two households beside; the Hontvet family at Smutty-Nose; and on Appledore, the household at the large house, and on the southern side, opposite Smutty-Nose, a little cottage, where lived Jorge Edvardt Ingebertsen, his wife and children, and several men who fished with him. Smutty-Nose is not in sight of the large house at Appledore, so we were in ignorance of all that happened on that dreadful night, longer than the other inhabitants of the Shoals.

John, Ivan, and Mathew went to draw their trawls, which had been set some miles to the eastward of the islands. They intended to be back to dinner, and then to go on to Portsmouth with their fish, and bait the trawls afresh, ready to bring back to set again next day. But the wind was strong and fair for Portsmouth and ahead for the island; it would have been a long beat home against it; so they went on to Portsmouth, without touching at the island to leave one man to guard the women, as had been their custom. This was the first night in all the years Maren had lived there that the house was without a man to protect it. But John, always thoughtful for her, asked Emil Ingebertsen, whom he met on the fishing-grounds, to go over from Appledore and tell her that they had gone on to Portsmouth with the favoring wind, but that they hoped to be back that night. And he would have been back had the bait he expected from Boston arrived on the train in which it was due. How curiously everything adjusted itself to favor the bringing about of this horrible catastrophe! The bait did not arrive till the half past twelve train, and they were obliged to work the whole night getting their trawls ready, thus leaving the way perfectly clear for Louis Wagner's awful work.

The three women left alone watched and waited in vain for the schooner to return, and kept the dinner hot for the men, and patiently wondered why they did not come. In vain they searched the wide horizon for that returning sail. Ah me, what pathos is in that longing look of women's eyes for far off sails! that gaze so eager, so steadfast, that it would almost seem as if it must conjure up the ghostly shape of glimmering canvas from the mysterious distances of sea and sky, and draw it unerringly home by the mere force of intense wistfulness! And those gentle eyes, that were never to see the light of another sun, looked anxiously across the heaving sea till twilight fell, and then John's messenger, Emil, arrived —Emil Ingebertsen, courteous and gentle as a youthful knight—and reassured them with his explanation, which having given, he departed, leaving them in a much more cheerful state of mind. So the three sisters, with only the little dog Ringe for a protector, sat by the fire chatting together cheerfully. They fully expected the schooner back again that night from Portsmouth, but they were not ill at ease while they waited. Of what should they be afraid? They had not an enemy in the world! No shadow crept to the fireside to warn them what was at hand, no portent of death chilled the air as they talked their pleasant talk and made their little plans in utter unconsciousness. Karen was to have gone to Portsmouth with the fishermen that day; she was all ready dressed to go. Various little commissions were given her, errands to do for the two sisters she was to leave behind. Maren wanted some buttons, and "I'll give you one for a pattern; I'll put it in your purse," she said to Karen, "and then when you open your purse you'll be sure to remember it." (That little button, of a peculiar pattern, was found in Wagner's possession afterward.) They sat up till ten o'clock, talking together. The night was bright and calm; it was a comfort to miss the bitter winds that had raved about the little dwelling all the long, rough winter. Already it was spring; this calm was the first token of its coming. It was the 6th of March; in a few weeks the weather would soften, the grass grow green, and Anethe would see the first flowers in this strange country, so far from her home where she had left father and mother, kith and kin, for love of Ivan. The delicious days of summer at hand would transform the work of the toiling fishermen to pleasure, and all things would bloom and smile about the poor people on the lonely rock! Alas, it was not to be.

At ten o'clock they went to bed. It was cold and "lonesome" up-stairs, so Maren put some chairs by the side of the lounge, laid a mattress upon it, and made up a bed for Karen in the kitchen, where she presently fell asleep. Maren and Anethe slept in the next room. So safe they felt themselves, they did not pull down a curtain, nor even try to fasten the house-door. They went to their rest in absolute security and perfect trust. It was the first still night of the new year; a young moon stole softly down toward the west, a gentle wind breathed through the quiet dark, and the waves whispered gently about the island, helping to lull those innocent souls to yet more peaceful slumber. Ah, where were the gales of March that night have plowed that tranquil sea to foam, and cut off the fatal path of Louis Wagner to that happy home! But nature seemed to pause and wait for him. I remember looking abroad over the waves that night and rejoicing over "the first calm night of the year!" It was so still, so bright! The hope of all the light and beauty a few weeks would bring forth stirred me to sudden joy. There should be spring again after the long winter weariness.

"Can trouble live in April days,
Or sadness in the summer moons?"

I thought, as I watched the clear sky, grown less hard than it had been for weeks, and sparkling with stars. But before another sunset it seemed to me that beauty had fled out of the world, and that goodness, innocence, mercy, gentleness, were a mere mockery of empty words.

Here let us leave the poor women, asleep on the lonely rock, with no help near them in heaven or upon earth, and follow the fishermen to Portsmouth, where they arrived about four o'clock that afternoon. One of the first men whom they saw as they neared the town was Louis Wagner; to him they threw the rope from the schooner, and he helped draw her in to the wharf. Greetings passed between them; he spoke to Mathew Hontvet, and as he looked at Ivan Christensen, the men noticed a flush pass over Louis's face. He asked were they going out again that night? Three times before they parted he asked that question; he saw that all the three men belonging to the island had come away together; he began to realize his opportunity. They answered him that if their bait came by the train in which they expected it, they hoped to get back that night, but if it was late they should be obliged to stay till morning, baiting their trawls; and they asked him to come and help them. It is a long and tedious business, the baiting of trawls; often more than a thousand hooks are to be manipulated, and lines and hooks coiled, clear of tangles, into tubs, all ready for throwing overboard when the fishing-grounds are reached. Louis gave them a half promise that he would help them, but they did not see him again after leaving the wharf. The three fishermen were hungry, not having touched at their island, where Maren always provided them with a supply of food to take with them; they asked each other if either had brought any money with which to buy bread, and it came out that every one had left his pocketbook at home. Louis, standing by, heard all this. He asked John, then, if he had made fishing pay. John answered that he had cleared about six hundred dollars.

The men parted, the honest three about their business; but Louis, what became of him with his evil thoughts? At about half past seven he went into a liquor shop and had a glass of something; not enough to make him unsteady,—he was too wise for that. He was not seen again in Portsmouth by any human creature that night. He must have gone, after that, directly down to the river, that beautiful, broad river, the Piscataqua, upon whose southern bank the quaint old city of Portsmouth dreams its quiet days away; and there he found a boat ready to his hand, a dory belonging to a man by the name of David Burke, who had that day furnished it with new thole-pins. When it was picked up afterward off the mouth of the river, Louis's anxious oars had eaten half-way through the substance of these pins, which are always made of the hardest, toughest wood that can be found. A terrible piece of rowing must that have been, in one night! Twelve miles from the city to the Shoals,— three to the light-houses, where the river meets the open sea, nine more to the islands; nine back again to Newcastle next morning! He took that boat, and with the favoring tide dropped down the rapid river where the swift current is so strong that oars are scarcely needed, except to keep the boat steady. Truly all nature seemed to play into his hands; this first relenting night of earliest spring favored him with its stillness, the tide was fair, the wind was fair, the little moon gave him just enough light, without betraying him to any curious eyes, as he glided down the three miles between the river banks, in haste to reach the sea. Doubtless the light west wind played about him as delicately as if he had been the most human of God's creatures; nothing breathed remonstrance in his ear, nothing whispered in the whispering water that rippled about his inexorable keel, steering straight for the Shoals through the quiet darkness. The snow lay thick and white upon the land in the moonlight; lamps twinkled here and there from dwellings on either side; in Eliot and Newcastle, in Portsmouth and Kittery, roofs, chimneys, and gables showed faintly in the vague light; the leafless trees clustered dark in hollows or lifted their tracery of bare boughs in higher spaces against the wintry sky. His eyes must have looked on it all, whether he saw the peaceful picture or not. Beneath many a humble roof honest folk were settling into their untroubled rest, as "this planned piece of deliberate wickedness" was stealing silently by with his heart full of darkness, blacker than the black tide that swirled beneath his boat and bore him fiercely on. At the river's mouth stood the sentinel light-houses, sending their great spokes of light afar into the night, like the arms of a wide humanity stretching into the darkness helping hands to bring all who needed succor safely home. He passed them, first the tower at Fort Point, then the taller one at Whale's Back, steadfastly holding aloft their warning fires. There was no signal from the warning bell as he rowed by, though a danger more subtle, more deadly, than fog, or hurricane, or pelting storm was passing swift beneath it. Unchallenged by anything in earth or heaven, he kept on his way and gained the great outer ocean, doubtless pulling strong and steadily, for he had no time to lose, and the longest night was all too short for an under taking such as this. Nine miles from the light-houses to the islands! Slowly he makes his way; it seems to take an eternity of time. And now he is midway between the islands and the coast. That little toy of a boat with its one occupant in the midst of the awful, black, heaving sea! The vast dim ocean whispers with a thousand waves; against the boat's side the ripples lightly tap, and pass and are lost; the air is full of fine, mysterious voices of winds and waters. Has he no fear, alone there on the midnight sea with such a purpose in his heart? The moonlight sends a long, golden track across the waves; it touches his dark face and figure, it glitters on his dripping oars. On his right hand Boone Island light shows like a setting star on the horizon, low on his left the two beacons twinkle off Newburyport, at the mouth of the Merrimack River; all the light-houses stand watching along the coast, wheeling their long, slender shafts of radiance as if pointing at this black atom creeping over the face of the planet with such colossal evil in his heart. Before him glitters the Shoals' light at White Island, and helps to guide him to his prey. Alas, my friendly light house, that you should serve so terrible a purpose! Steadily the oars click in the rowlocks; stroke after stroke of the broad blades draws him away from the lessening line of land, over the wavering floor of the ocean, nearer the lonely rocks. Slowly the coast-lights fade, and now the rote of the sea among the lonely ledges of the Shoals salutes his attentive ear. A little longer and he nears Appledore, the first island, and now he passes by the snow-covered, ice-bound rock, with the long buildings showing clear in the moonlight. He must have looked at them as he went past. I wonder we who slept beneath the roofs that glimmered to his eyes in the uncertain light did not feel, through the thick veil of sleep, what fearful thing passed by! But we slumbered peacefully as the unhappy women whose doom every click of those oars in the rowlocks, like the ticking of some dreadful clock, was bringing nearer and nearer. Between the islands he passes; they are full of chilly gleams and glooms. There is no scene more weird than these snow-covered rocks in winter, more shudderful and strange: the moonlight touching them with mystic glimmer, the black water breaking about them and the vast shadowy spaces of the sea stretching to the horizon on every side, full of vague sounds, of half lights and shadows, of fear, and of mystery. The island he seeks lies before him, lone and still; there is no gleam in any window, there is no help near, nothing upon which the women can call for succor. He does not land in the cove where all boats put in, he rows round to the south side and draws his boat up on the rocks. His red returning footsteps are found here next day, staining the snow. He makes his way to the house he knows so well.

All is silent: nothing moves, nothing sounds but the hushed voices of the sea. His hand is on the latch, he enters stealthily, there is nothing to resist him. The little dog, Ringe, begins to bark sharp and loud, and Karen rouses, crying, "John, is that you?" thinking the expected fishermen had returned. Louis seizes a chair and strikes at her in the dark; the clock on a shelf above her head falls down with the jarring of the blow, and stops at exactly seven minutes to one. Maren in the next room, waked suddenly from her sound sleep, trying in vain to make out the meaning of it all, cries, "What's the matter?" Karen answers, "John scared me!" Maren springs from her bed and tries to open her chamber door; Louis has fastened it on the other side by pushing a stick through the latch. With her heart leaping with terror the poor child shakes the door with all her might, in vain. Utterly confounded and bewildered, she hears Karen screaming, "John kills me! John kills me!" She hears the sound of repeated blows and shrieks, till at last her sister falls heavily against the door, which gives way, and Maren rushes out. She catches dimly a glimpse of a tall figure outlined against the southern window; she seizes poor Karen and drags her with the strength of frenzy within the bedroom. This unknown terror, this fierce, dumb monster who never utters a sound to betray himself through the whole, pursues her with blows, strikes her three times with a chair, either blow with fury sufficient to kill her, had it been light enough for him to see how to direct it; but she gets her sister inside and the door shut, and holds it against him with all her might and Karen's failing strength. What a little heroine was this poor child, struggling with the force of desperation to save herself and her sisters!

All this time Anethe lay dumb, not daring to move or breathe, roused from the deep sleep of youth and health by this nameless, formless terror. Maren, while she strives to hold the door at which Louis rattles again and again, calls to her in anguish, "Anethe, Anethe! Get out of the window! run! hide!" The poor girl, almost paralyzed with fear, tries to obey, puts her bare feet out of the low window, and stands outside in the freezing snow, with one light garment over her cowering figure, shrinking in the cold winter wind, the clear moonlight touching her white face and bright hair and fair young shoulders. "Scream! scream!" shouts frantic Maren. "Somebody at Star Island may hear!" but Anethe answers with the calmness of despair, "I cannot make a sound." Maren screams, herself, but the feeble sound avails nothing. "Run! run!" she cries to Anethe; but again Anethe answers, "I cannot move."

Louis has left off trying to force the door; he listens. Are the women trying to escape? He goes out of doors. Maren flies to the window; he comes round the corner of the house and confronts Anethe where she stands in the snow. The moonlight shines full in his face; she shrieks loudly and distinctly, "Louis, Louis!" Ah, he is discovered, he is recognized! Quick as thought he goes back to the front door, at the side of which stands an ax, left there by Maren, who had used it the day before to cut the ice from the well. He returns to Anethe standing shuddering there. It is no matter that she is beautiful, young, and helpless to resist, that she has been kind to him, that she never did a human creature harm, that she stretches her gentle hands out to him in agonized entreaty, crying piteously, "Oh, Louis, Louis, Louis!" He raises the ax and brings it down on her bright head in one tremendous blow, and she sinks without a sound and lies in a heap, with her warm blood reddening the snow. Then he deals her blow after blow, almost within reach of Maren's hands, as she stands at the window. Distracted, Maren strives to rouse poor Karen, who kneels with her head on the side of the bed; with desperate entreaty she tries to get her up and away, but Karen moans, "I cannot, I cannot." She is too far gone; and then Maren knows she cannot save her, and that she must flee herself or die. So, while Louis again enters the house, she seizes a skirt and wraps round her shoulders, and makes her way out of the open window, over Anethe's murdered body, barefooted, flying away, anywhere, breathless, shaking with terror.

Where can she go? Her little dog, frightened into silence, follows her,—pressing so close to her feet that she falls over him more than once. Looking back she sees Louis has lit a lamp and is seeking for her. She flies to the cove; if she can but find his boat and row away in it and get help! It is not there; there is no boat in which she can get away. She hears Karen's wild screams, he is killing her! Oh where can she go? Is there any place on that little island where he will not find her? She thinks she will creep into one of the empty old houses by the water; but no, she reflects, if I hide there, Ringe will bark and betray me the moment Louis comes to look for me. And Ringe saved her life, for next day Louis's bloody tracks were found all about those old buildings where he had sought her. She flies, with Karen's awful cries in her ears, away over rocks and snow to the farthest limit she can gain. The moon has set; it is about two o'clock in the morning, and oh, so cold! She shivers and shudders from head to feet, but her agony of terror is so great she is hardly conscious of bodily sensation. And welcome is the freezing snow, the jagged ice and iron rocks that tear her unprotected feet, the bitter brine that beats against the shore, the winter winds that make her shrink and tremble; "they are not so unkind as man's ingratitude!" Falling often, rising, struggling on with feverish haste, she makes her way to the very edge of the water; down almost into the sea she creeps, between two rocks, upon her hands and knees, and crouches, face downward, with Ringe nestled close beneath her breast, not daring to move through the long hours that must pass before the sun will rise again. She is so near the ocean she can almost reach the water with her hand. Had the wind breathed the least roughly the waves must have washed over her. There let us leave her and go back to Louis Wagner. Maren heard her sister Karen's shrieks as she fled. The poor girl had crept into an unoccupied room in a distant part of the house, striving to hide herself. He could not kill her with blows, blundering in the darkness, so he wound a handkerchief about her throat and strangled her. But now he seeks anxiously for Maren. Has she escaped? What terror is in the thought! Escaped, to tell the tale, to accuse him as the murderer of her sisters. Hurriedly, with desperate anxiety, he seeks for her. His time was growing short; it was not in his programme that this brave little creature should give him so much trouble; he had not calculated on resistance from these weak and helpless women. Already it was morning, soon it would be daylight. He could not find her in or near the house;

he went down to the empty and dilapidated houses about the cove, and sought her everywhere. What a picture! That blood-stained butcher, with his dark face, crawling about those cellars, peering for that woman! He dared not spend any more time; he must go back for the money he hoped to find, his reward for this! All about the house he searches, in bureau drawers, in trunks and boxes: he finds fifteen dollars for his night's work! Several hundreds were lying between some sheets folded at the bottom of a drawer in which he looked. But he cannot stop for more thorough investigation; a dreadful haste pursues him like a thousand fiends. He drags Anethe's stiffening body into the house, and leaves it on the kitchen floor. If the thought crosses his mind to set fire to the house and burn up his two victims, he dares not do it: it will make a fatal bon fire to light his homeward way; besides, it is useless, for Maren has escaped to accuse him, and the time presses so horribly! But how cool a monster is he! After all this hard work he must have refreshment to support him in the long row back to the land; knife and fork, cup and plate, were found next morning on the table near where Anethe lay; fragments of food which was not cooked in the house, but brought from Portsmouth, were scattered about. Tidy Maren had left neither dishes nor food when they went to bed. The handle of the tea-pot which she had left on the stove was stained and smeared with blood. Can the human mind conceive of such hideous nonchalance? Wagner sat down in that room and ate and drank! It is almost beyond belief! Then he went to the well with a basin and towels, tried to wash off the blood, and left towels and basin in the well. He knows he must be gone! It is certain death to linger. He takes his boat and rows away toward the dark coast and the twinkling lights; it is for dear life, now! What powerful strokes send the small skiff rushing over the water!

There is no longer any moon, the night is far spent; already the east changes, the stars fade; he rows like a madman to reach the land, but a blush of morning is stealing up the sky and sunrise is rosy over shore and sea, when panting, trembling, weary, a creature accursed, a blot on the face of the day, he lands at Newcastle—too late! Too late! In vain he casts the dory adrift; she will not float away; the flood tide bears her back to give her testimony against him, and afterward she is found at Jaffrey's Point, near the "Devil's Den," and the fact of her worn thole-pins noted. Wet, covered with ice from the spray which has flown from his eager oars, utterly exhausted, he creeps to a knoll and reconnoitres; he thinks he is unobserved, and crawls on towards Portsmouth. But he is seen and recognized by many persons, and his identity established beyond a doubt. He goes to the house of Mathew Jonsen, where he has been living, steals up-stairs, changes his clothes, and appears before the family, anxious, frightened, agitated, telling Jonsen he never felt so badly in his life; that he has got into trouble and is afraid he shall be taken. He cannot eat at breakfast, says "farewell forever," goes away and is shaved, and takes the train to Boston, where he provides himself with new clothes, shoes, a complete outfit, but lingering, held by fate, he cannot fly, and before night the officer's hand is on his shoulder and he is arrested.

Meanwhile poor shuddering Maren on the lonely island, by the water-side, waits till the sun is high in heaven before she dares come forth. She thinks he may be still on the island. She said to me, "I thought he must be there, dead or alive. I thought he might go crazy and kill himself after having done all that." At last she steals out. The little dog frisks before her; it is so cold her feet cling to the rocks and snow at every step, till the skin is fairly torn off. Still and frosty is the bright morning, the water lies smiling and sparkling, the hammers of the workmen building the new hotel on Star Island sound through the quiet air. Being on the side of Smutty-Nose opposite Star, she waves her skirt, and screams to attract their attention; they hear her, turn and look, see a woman waving a signal of distress, and, surprising to relate, turn tranquilly to their work again. She realizes at last there is no hope in that direction; she must go round toward Appledore in sight of the dreadful house. Passing it afar off she gives one swift glance toward it, terrified lest in the broad sunshine she may see some horrid token of last night's work; but all is still and peaceful. She notices the curtains the three had left up when they went to bed; they are now drawn down; she knows whose hand has done this, and what it hides from the light of day. Sick at heart, she makes her painful way to the northern edge of Malaga, which is connected with Smutty-Nose by the old sea-wall. She is directly opposite Appledore and the little cottage where abide her friend and countryman, Jorge Edvardt Ingebertsen, and his wife and children. Only a quarter of a mile of the still ocean separates her from safety and comfort. She sees the children playing about the door; she calls and calls. Will no one ever hear her? Her torn feet torment her, she is sore with blows and perishing with cold. At last her voice reaches the ears of the children, who run and tell their father that some one is crying and calling; looking across, he sees the poor little figure waving her arms, takes his dory and paddles over, and with amazement recognizes Maren in her night-dress, with bare feet and streaming hair, with a cruel bruise upon her face, with wild eyes, distracted, half senseless with cold and terror. He cries, "Maren, Maren, who has done this? what is it? who is it?" and her only answer is "Louis, Louis, Louis!" as he takes her on board his boat and rows home with her as fast as he can. From her incoherent statement he learns what has happened. Leaving her in the care of his family, he comes over across the hill to the great house on Appledore. As I sit at my desk I see him pass the window, and wonder why the old man comes so fast and anxiously through the heavy snow.

Presently I see him going back again, accompanied by several of his own countrymen and others of our workmen, carrying guns. They are going to Smutty-Nose, and take arms, thinking it possible Wagner may yet be there. I call down-stairs, "What has happened?" and am answered, "Some trouble at Smutty-Nose; we hardly understand." "Probably a drunken brawl of the reckless fishermen who may have landed there," I say to myself, and go on with my work. In another half-hour I see the men returning, reinforced by others, coming fast, confusedly; and suddenly a wail of anguish comes up from the women below. I cannot believe it when I hear them crying, "Karen is dead! Anethe is dead! Louis Wagner has murdered them both!" I run out into the servants' quarters; there are all the men assembled, an awe-stricken crowd. Old Ingebertsen comes forward and tells me the bare facts and how Maren lies at his house, half crazy, suffering with her torn and frozen feet. Then the men are dispatched to search Appledore, to find if by any chance the murderer might be concealed about the place, and I go over to Maren to see if I can do anything for her. I find the women and children with frightened faces at the little cottage; as I go into the room where Maren lies, she catches my hands, crying, "Oh, I so glad to see you! I so glad I save my life!" and with her dry lips she tells me all the story as I have told it here. Poor little creature, holding me with those wild, glittering', dilated eyes, she cannot tell me rapidly enough the whole horrible tale. Upon her cheek is yet the blood-stain from the blow he struck her with a chair, and she shows me two more upon her shoulder, and her torn feet. I go back for arnica with which to bathe them. What a mockery seems to me the "jocund day" as I emerge into the sun shine, and looking across the space of blue, sparkling water, see the house wherein all that horror lies!

Oh brightly shines the morning sun and glitters on the white sails of the little vessel that comes dancing back from Portsmouth before the favoring wind, with the two husbands on board! How glad they are for the sweet morning and the fair wind that brings them home again! And Ivan sees in fancy Anethe's face all beautiful with welcoming smiles, and John knows how happy his good and faithful Maren will be to see him back again. Alas, how little they dream what lies before them! From Appledore they are signaled to come ashore, and Ivan and Mathew, landing, hear a confused rumor of trouble from tongues that hardly can frame the words that must tell the dreadful truth. Ivan only understands that something is wrong. His one thought is for Anethe; he flies to Ingebertsen's cottage, she may be there; he rushes in like a maniac, crying, "Anethe, Anethe! Where is Anethe?" and broken-hearted Maren answers her brother, "Anethe is—at home." He does not wait for another word, but seizes the little boat and lands at the same time with John on Smutty-Nose; with headlong haste they reach the house, other men accompanying them; ah, there are blood-stains all about the snow! Ivan is the first to burst open the door and enter. What words can tell it! There upon the floor, naked, stiff, and stark, is the woman he idolizes, for whose dear feet he could not make life's ways smooth and pleasant enough—stone dead! Dead—horribly butchered! her bright hair stiff with blood, the fair head that had so often rested on his breast crushed! cloven, mangled with the brutal ax! Their eyes are blasted by the intolerable sight: both John and Ivan stagger out and fall, senseless, in the snow. Poor Ivan! his wife a thousand times adored, the dear girl he had brought from Norway, the good, sweet; girl who loved him so, whom he could not cherish tenderly enough! And he was not there to protect her! There was no one there to save her!

"Did Heaven look on
And would not take their part!"

Poor fellow, what had he done that fate should deal him such a blow as this! Dumb, blind with anguish, he made no sign.

"What says the body when they spring
Some monstrous torture engine's whole
Strength on it? No more says the soul."

Some of his pitying comrades lead him away, like one stupefied, and take him back to Appledore. John knows his wife is safe. Though stricken with horror and consumed with wrath, he is not paralyzed like poor Ivan, who has been smitten with worse than death. They find Karen's body in another part of the house, covered with blows and black in the face, strangled. They find Louis's tracks,—all the tokens of his disastrous presence,—the contents of trunks and drawers scattered about in his hasty search for the money, and, all within the house and without, blood, blood everywhere.

When I reach the cottage with the arnica for Maren, they have returned from Smutty-Nose. John, her husband, is there. He is a young man of the true Norse type, blue eyed, fair-haired, tall and well-made, with handsome teeth and bronzed beard. Perhaps he is a little quiet and undemonstrative generally, but at this moment he is superb, kindled from head to feet, a fire-brand of woe and wrath, with eyes that flash and cheeks that burn. I speak a few words to him,—what words can meet such an occasion as this! — and having given directions about the use of the arnica, for Maren, I go away, for nothing more can be done for her, and every comfort she needs is hers. The outer room is full of men; they make way for me, and as I pass through I catch a glimpse of Ivan crouched with his arms thrown round his knees and his head bowed down between them, motionless, his attitude expressing such abandonment of despair as cannot be described. His whole person seems to shrink, as if deprecating the blow that has fallen upon him.

All day the slaughtered women lie as they were found, for nothing can be touched till the officers of the law have seen the whole. And John goes back to Portsmouth to tell his tale to the proper authorities. What a different voyage from the one he had just taken, when happy and careless he was returning to the home he had left so full of peace and comfort! What a load he bears back with him, as he makes his tedious way across the miles that separate him from the means of vengeance he burns to reach! But at last he arrives, tells his story, the police at other cities are at once telegraphed, and the city marshal follows Wagner to Boston. At eight o'clock that evening comes the steamer Mayflower to the Shoals, with all the officers on board. They land and make investigations at Smutty-Nose, then come here to Appledore and examine Maren, and, when everything is done, steam back to Portsmouth, which they reach at three o'clock in the morning. After all are gone and his awful day's work is finished at last, poor John comes back to Maren, and kneeling by the side of her bed, he is utterly overpowered with what he has passed through; he is shaken with sobs as he cries, "Oh, Maren, Maren, it is too much, too much! I cannot bear it!" And Maren throws her arms about his neck, crying, "Oh, John, John, don't! I shall be crazy, I shall die, if you go on like that." Poor innocent, unhappy people, who never wronged a fellow-creature in their lives!

But Ivan—what is their anguish to his! They dare not leave him alone lest he do himself an injury. He is perfectly mute and listless; he cannot weep, he can neither eat nor sleep. He sits like one in a horrid dream. "Oh, my poor, poor brother!" Maren cries in tones of deepest grief, when I speak his name to her next day. She herself cannot rest a moment till she hears that Louis is taken; at every sound her crazed imagination fancies he is coming back for her; she is fairly beside herself with terror and anxiety; but the night following that of the catastrophe brings us news that he is arrested, and there is stern rejoicing at the Shoals; but no vengeance taken on him can bring back those un-offending lives, or restore that gentle home. The dead are properly cared for; the blood is washed from Anethe's beautiful bright hair; she is clothed in her wedding-dress, the blue dress in which she was married, poor child, that happy Christmas time in Norway, a little more than a year ago. They are carried across the sea to Portsmouth, the burial service is read over them, and they are hidden in the earth. After poor Ivan has seen the faces of his wife and sister still and pale in their coffins, their ghastly wounds concealed as much as possible, flowers upon them and the priest praying over them, his trance of misery is broken, the grasp of despair is loosened a little about his heart. Yet hardly does he notice whether the sun shines or no, or care whether he lives or dies. Slowly his senses steady themselves from the effects of a shock that nearly destroyed him, and merciful time, with imperceptible touch, softens day by day the outlines of that picture at the memory of which he will never cease to shudder while he lives.

Louis Wagner was captured in Boston on the evening of the next day after his atrocious deed, and Friday morning, followed by a hooting mob, he was taken to the Eastern depot. At every station along the route crowds were assembled, and there were fierce cries for vengeance. At the depot in Portsmouth a dense crowd of thousands of both sexes had gathered, who assailed him with yells and curses and cries of "Tear him to pieces!" It was with difficulty he was at last safely imprisoned. Poor Maren was taken to Portsmouth from Appledore on that day. The story of Wagner's day in Boston, like every other detail of the affair, has been told by every newspaper in the country: his agitation and restlessness, noted by all who saw him; his curious, reckless talk. To one he says, "I have just killed two sailors;" to another, Jacob Toldtman, into whose shop he goes to buy shoes, "I have seen a woman lie as still as that boot," and so on. When he is caught he puts on a bold face and determines to brave it out; denies everything with tears and virtuous indignation. The men whom he has so fearfully wronged are confronted with him; his attitude is one of injured innocence; he surveys them more in sorrow than in anger, while John is on fire with wrath and indignation, and hurls maledictions at him; but Ivan, poor Ivan, hurt beyond all hope or help, is utterly mute; he does not utter one word. Of what use is it to curse the murderer of his wife? It will not bring her back; he has no heart for cursing, he is too completely broken. Maren told me the first time she was brought into Louis's presence, her heart leaped so fast she could hardly breathe. She entered the room softly with her husband and Mathew Jonsen's daughter. Louis was whittling a stick. He looked up and saw her face, and the color ebbed out of his, and rushed back and stood in one burning spot in his cheek, as he looked at her and she looked at him for a space, in silence. Then he drew about his evil mind the detestable garment of sanctimoniousness, and in sentimental accents he murmured, "I'm glad Jesus loves me!" "The devil loves you!" cried John, with uncompromising veracity. "I know it wasn't nice," said decorous Maren, "but John couldn't help it; it was too much to bear!"

The next Saturday afternoon, when he was to be taken to Saco, hundreds of fishermen came to Portsmouth from all parts of the coast, determined on his destruction, and there was a fearful scene in the quiet streets of that peaceful city when he was being escorted to the train by the police and various officers of justice. Two thousand people had assembled, and such a furious, yelling crowd was never seen or heard in Portsmouth. The air was rent with cries for vengeance; showers of bricks and stones were thrown from all directions, and wounded several of the officers who surrounded Wagner. His knees trembled under him, he shook like an aspen, and the officers found it necessary to drag him along, telling him he must keep up if he would save his life. Except that they feared to injure the innocent as well as the guilty, those men would have literally torn him to pieces. But at last he was put on board the cars in safety, and carried away to prison. His demeanor throughout the term of his confinement, and during his trial and subsequent imprisonment, was a wonderful piece of acting. He really inspired people with doubt as to his guilt. I make an extract from The Portsmouth Chronicle, dated March l3, 1873: "Wagner still retains his amazing sang froid, which is wonderful, even in a strong-nerved German. The sympathy of most of the visitors at his jail has certainly been won by his calmness and his general appearance, which is quite prepossessing." This little instance of his method of proceeding I must subjoin: A lady who had come to converse with him on the subject of his eternal salvation said, as she left him, "I hope you put your trust in the Lord," to which he sweetly answered, "I always did, ma'am, and I always shall."

A few weeks after all this had happened, I sat by the window one afternoon, and, looking up from my work, I saw some one passing slowly,—a young man who seemed so thin, so pale, so bent and ill, that I said, "Here is some stranger who is so very sick, he is probably come to try the effect of the air, even thus early." It was Ivan Christensen. I did not recognize him. He dragged one foot after the other wearily, and walked with the feeble motion of an old man. He entered the house; his errand was to ask for work. He could not bear to go away from the neighborhood of the place where Anethe had lived and where they had been so happy, and he could not bear to work at fishing on the south side of the island, within sight of that house. There was work enough for him here; a kind voice told him so, a kind hand was laid on his shoulder, and he was bidden come and welcome. The tears rushed into the poor fellow's eyes, he went hastily away, and that night sent over his chest of tools,—he was a carpenter by trade. Next day he took up his abode here and worked all summer. Every day I carefully observed him as I passed him by, regarding him with an inexpressible pity, of which he was perfectly unconscious, as he seemed to be of everything and everybody. He never raised his head when he answered my "Good morning," or "Good evening, Ivan." Though I often wished to speak, I never said more to him, for he seemed to me to be hurt too sorely to be touched by human hand. With his head sunk on his breast, and wearily dragging his limbs, he pushed the plane or drove the saw to and fro with a kind of dogged persistence, looking neither to the left nor right. Well might the weight of woe he carried bow him to the earth! By and by he spoke, himself, to other members of the household, saying, with a patient sorrow, he believed it was to have been, it had been so ordered, else why did all things so play into Louis's hands? All things were furnished him: the knowledge of the unprotected state of the women, a perfectly clear field in which to carry out his plans, just the right boat he wanted in which to make his voyage, fair tide, fair wind, calm sea, just moonlight enough; even the ax with which to kill Anethe stood ready to his hand at the house door. Alas, it was to have been! Last summer Ivan went back again to Norway—alone. Hardly is it probable that he will ever return to a land whose welcome to him fate made so horrible. His sister Maren and her husband still live blameless lives, with the little dog Ringe, in a new home they have made for themselves in Portsmouth, not far from the river side; the merciful lapse of days and years takes them gently but surely away from the thought of that season of anguish; and though they can never forget it all, they have grown resigned and quiet again. And on the island other Norwegians have settled, voices of charming children sound sweetly in the solitude that echoed so awfully to the shrieks of Karen and Maren. But to the weirdness of the winter midnight something is added, a vision of two dim, reproachful shades who watch while an agonized ghost prowls eternally about the dilapidated houses at the beach's edge, close by the black, whispering water, seeking for the woman who has escaped him—escaped to bring upon him the death he deserves, whom he never, never, never can find, though his distracted spirit may search till man shall vanish from off the face of the earth, and time shall be no more.

Made in the USA
Monee, IL
16 February 2023

28023194R00056